VILFREDO PARETO

CLASSICS IN THE HISTORY AND DEVELOPMENT OF ECONOMICS

General Editor: **Michio Morishima**, Emeritus Professor of Economics,
London School of Economics

In the postwar years the discipline of economics has become highly advanced by focusing upon issues which can be expressed in mathematical terms and ignoring issues upon which it is difficult to make axiomatic analysis. This series aims to make available in English texts which might well have played a major role in the development of a more balanced – not exclusively mathematical – economic theory but for the fact that they were written in a language other than English. However, the series' interest will also embrace mathematical and English-language works where these appear to have been unduly neglected. The series will also seek to make available in English important works that present the experiences of non-English-speaking economies; it is hoped that these will contribute greatly to making economics more comprehensive and more widely applicable to a range of world economies in the future.

Alfonso de Pietri-Tonelli and Georges H. Bousquet
VILFREDO PARETO: NEOCLASSICAL SYNTHESIS OF ECONOMICS AND
SOCIOLOGY

Hiroshi Hazama
THE HISTORY OF LABOUR MANAGEMENT IN JAPAN

Giulio La Volpe
STUDIES ON THE THEORY OF GENERAL DYNAMIC ECONOMIC EQUILIBRIUM

Hiroshi Okumura
JAPANESE CORPORATION CAPITALISM

Yasuma Takata
POWER THEORY OF ECONOMICS

Vilfredo Pareto
Neoclassical Synthesis of Economics and Sociology

Alfonso de Pietri-Tonelli
sometime Professor of Economic Policy
University of Venice

and

Georges H. Bousquet
sometime Professor
University of Algiers and University of Bordeaux

Translated by
Julia Bamford, Laura Rival and Jonathan Steele

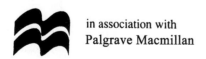

in association with
Palgrave Macmillan

First published 1994 by
THE MACMILLAN PRESS LTD
Houndmills, Basingstoke, Hampshire RG21 2XS
and London
Companies and representatives
throughout the world

ISBN 978-1-349-13324-6   ISBN 978-1-349-13322-2 (eBook)
DOI 10.1007/978-1-349-13322-2
A catalogue record for this book is available
from the British Library.

Contents

Series Editor's Introduction	vii
Note on the Authors	ix
Foreword by Michio Morishima	xi
List of Abbreviations	xxvii
1 A Short Biography *Alfonso de Pietri-Tonelli*	1
2 The Economist *Alfonso de Pietri-Tonelli*	5
3 Pareto's General Equilibrium Equations *Alfonso de Pietri-Tonelli*	21
4 Pareto and Socialism *Georges H. Bousquet*	29
5 The Sociologist *Georges H. Bousquet*	41
6 Pareto and the Problems of Modern Society *Georges H. Bousquet*	61
7 Fascism and the Impartial Theoretician *Alfonso de Pietri-Tonelli*	75
8 In the Decade after his Death *Alfonso de Pietri-Tonelli*	91
Translators: Chapters 1,2,3,7,8 – Julia Bamford Chapters 4,5,6 – Laura Rival and Jonathan Steele	
Notes	117
Index	123

Series Editor's Introduction

This series, with its designation 'for the development of economics' has at least four areas of focus, though it would be too restrictive to call them aims.

Since the last war economics has become 'mathematicized' to what could be deemed an excessive degree, so much so that mathematical models are incorporated into the analysis even of questions where there is no need for mathematical argument. As a result, those issues which cannot be expressed in mathematical terms have been all but forgotten. Moreover it has become almost impossible to establish links between economics and other social sciences, in which mathematics are little used. This increasing use of mathematics has thus meant that economics has become isolated; the isolation has in its turn promoted mathematical inbreeding.

The net result is that the discipline of economics has lost many of the capabilities which it formerly possessed. Moreover, since such capabilities have been dispensed with in the selection of specialists, it has become more and more difficult to shift economics away from the path along which it is now proceeding.

One effective means of correcting this tendency, and of giving the contents of economics a better balance, is to dig out some of the economics of the past, and to learn again from those who have gone before us. In the earlier decades of this century economics was not the overwhelmingly English language dominated discipline that it has become in the postwar period. There were top-class economics achievements in French, German, Italian and other languages as well. My intention, therefore, is to select from the papers and books written in other languages some which I consider to contain useful knowledge and suggestions, which may help to promote a more balanced economic theory. By translating these works into English, they will be made available to all. This is the first point we will take account of. Secondly, I will try to annex to the series wherever possible critical biographies of scholars active in a wide variety of fields, apart from mathematical economics, in order better to learn from them.

This series is not, however, necessarily 'anti-mathematical'. It is also the intention to include in the series works which might well have played a major role in the mainstream development of economics in the postwar years but the misfortune that they were written in a language other than

English has caused them to remain unknown. This, therefore, is the third point we have in mind.

Finally, modern national economies have not all evolved in an identical fashion. In Japan, for example, and in some other non-English-speaking economies, there have developed perfectly viable and, indeed, efficient economic systems. Work to clarify the structures of these kinds of economic system has been accumulating, but mostly in the language of the country itself. I am also anxious, therefore, to incorporate into the series translations of works in this area, and also research on the historical experience of these economies.

Given the four areas of focus which I have outlined above, the series as a whole will inevitably have a somewhat 'motley' character. While the works may be somewhat disparate, though, I want to build up a series in which all the volumes will prove enjoyable and interesting to read. The endeavour involves a great deal of translation work, meaning that publication at regular intervals is likely to be impossible. In addition, there are many candidates whose work must be considered for inclusion. This, of course, makes a great deal of work for a single editor, and therefore it will take time for him to put the project into orbit. My fervent hope, however, is that this series, which, among other things, expresses my own philosophy on the need for a more balanced economics, will succeed in arousing the interest of both students and specialists in a wider economics, and educating them in that economics.

MICHIO MORISHIMA

Note on the Authors

Alfonso de Pietri-Tonelli

Born in Carpi, Italy, in 1883, Alfonso de Pietri-Tonelli graduated in economics in 1906 at the University of Venice. There he became Professor of Political Economy in 1923, a post he held until his death in 1952.

After a few years of passionate interest in labour organisations, Marxism and Malthusianism, he finally devoted himself to the study of economics using mathematical methodologies, following Pareto.

His most valuable contributions include: general studies on political economy, conceived as a rational synthesis of political theory and economics (*Corso di politica economica*, 1927); innovative generalisation of equilibrium theorems by Cournot, Walras and Pareto (*Traité d'Economie rationelle*, 1927; *Prospetto dell'economia matematica*, 1930); a rigorous theory of political behaviour (*Teoria matematica delle scelte politiche*, 1943); analytical studies on stock market speculators (*La Spéculation de Bourse*, 1924); essays on fiscal policies (*L'inflazione fiscale in Italia*, 1951).

Apart from his many books and articles, his critical acumen emerged clearly from his reviews, a regular feature of the academic journal *Rivista di politica economica* for almost thirty years.

Georges H. Bousquet

Georges H. Bousquet (1900–78) started his career as Professor of Comparative Islamic Law and North African Sociology of the French Law Faculty of Algiers. He developed a keen interest in the history of mathematical economics and moved to France as professor at the University of Bordeaux. There he soon became a well-known economist and sociologist, with a very long association with the journal *Revue d'Economie politique*.

He was a great admirer of Vilfredo Pareto, whom he befriended, and greatly contributed to the knowledge of Pareto's theories in France.

Bousquet's main works are *Essai sur l'évolution de la pensée économique* (1927), *Cours d'économie pure* (1928), *Esquisse d'une histoire de la science économique en Italie* (1960).

Foreword

I

If we take the view that economics is part of a single whole along with the other social sciences (for example, sociology), it must be considered that there are key thinkers – Marx, Pareto, Weber and Schumpeter. In the case of Marx the social philosophy of historical materialism is synthesised with Marxian economics, while Pareto's own sociology is one with the so-called Walras-Pareto theory of general equilibrium. Leaving aside its methodology, Pareto's sociology consists mainly of a theory of the general form of society, a theory of social equilibrium and a theory of class circulation concerned with the decline of the ruling class and the change in the form of society which accompanies it. This means that Pareto's theories as a whole take on the form of a spectacular equilibrium theory of both society and the economy. Of course, the concept of equilibrium found in his economic theory comes from classical mechanics, while that in the social theory is more related to the concept of equilibrium of statistical mechanics, so it is not an easy thing to achieve a harmonious coexistence between these different equilibria. What I want to do in this introduction is to look generally at the Marxian synthesis and the Pareto-type synthesis, and in doing so to clarify the characteristics of the latter. At the same time I hope that it will provide some insights to those with an interest in the multi-disciplinarisation of economics.

II

Pareto devised a scrupulous methodology in order to construct the kind of synthesised theory he desired. He took the view that human behaviour is not necessarily logical. This results from the fact that neither individuals nor groups always act according to their own particular principles. In many cases their desires and decisions are formulated impulsively, emotionally or illogically. Where they do act in accordance with certain principles, an analysis of the kind of action implied or rejected by those principles enables clarification of the kind of action taken or never taken by both groups and individuals. Economics assumes that individual and collective actions result from the rational pursuit in this sense of certain principles – rational in the sense of utility or profit calculation – and the theory is constructed on this assumption. However, not all economic activity is logical and based on specific principles. (For example, a worker's decision whether or not to strike is never made purely in this logical manner.) Economics is totally inadequate when it comes to dealing with economic actions resulting from non-logical decision-making. It is assumed that none of these actions has any economic significance, and economists have developed their discipline as a kind of economic geometry whose basic axioms are the economic principles of the individual and the firm.

In non-logical actions an important role is played by human sentiment, human feelings and human emotions. Action based on utility and profit calculation (which I call economic actions in the narrow sense) is logical, while other, non-routine economic actions – for example those resulting from an upsurge in labour movements such as strike decisions or others which are affected differently according to political circumstances – (referred to as economic actions in the broad sense) are not necessarily logical. Moreover, behind new economic plans relating to innovation we find inspiration, vision and motivation of the innovator. Should we fail to understand this, and try to explain new projects purely in terms of utility or profit analysis, we will end up failing to recognise their true nature and their significance.

By contrast Marx took a different view, namely that relations of production or an economic structure lay at the root of society. On this basis was constructed a political and legal system, and a spiritual life (religion, morality, scholarship, the arts, etc.) developed. The various systems and spiritual life constructed on this economic foundation were termed the superstructure. Seen from this perspective the fundamental economic relations and activities of society – if we exclude economic activity in the broad sense – are seen to be logical, while those phenomena occurring in the superstructure are mainly non-logical.

Both economic action in the narrow sense and that in the broad sense are inherent in the sphere of economics. However, we have in addition actions in other areas not directly related to the economy, such as law, politics, religion and culture – actions in those areas referred to by Marx and Engels as the superstructure. Pareto regarded activities of this kind as being in principle non-logical. Pareto recognised the existence of economic action in the broad sense of the term, but his analysis of that particular area remained incomplete. For that reason his economics consisted mainly of a theory of logical action, hence for him the problem of synthesising economics and other social sciences was essentially the problem of how to bring together the analysis of logical action and the analysis of non-logical, non-economic activities.

III

Now for Marx, the relationship between the basic structure and the superstructure was in principle a one-sided one. If the basic structure changed, then the superstructure would change accordingly, while by contrast changes in the superstructure would not lead to appropriate changes in the foundation structure. Even if there were any such changes, they would be insignificant. Any reverse influence from the superstructure to the substructure could thus be disregarded. If we accept the existence of this kind of one-sided structural relationship proposed by Marx, then economics – the study of the foundation structure – effectively remains the study of logical action, and there is no need to deal with non-logical actions whose economic significance is negligible.

However, as Max Weber has made clear,[1] where religion influences the mode of people's economic activity – and as has recently become apparent in the countries of Eastern Europe and the former Soviet Union, if there is a change in a people's value system – the economic structure also ends up changing accordingly. Given that, the relationship between the foundations and the superstructure is clearly not a one-sided one, but a two-way one. Pareto, too, believed the relationship to be a two-way one. This being the case, economics must come together with those disciples concerned with the superstructure to create 'a far broader economics'. The above-mentioned equilibrium theory relating to both economy and society is just such a theory.

In Marx the appearance of historical materialism is premised in the one-way relationship between the superstructure and the foundation. According to this basic assumption productive forces determine the relations of production, and the superstructural phenomenon we call ideology is also determined in accordance with the relations of production. If, by contrast, we reject this assumption, then ideology and religion – as asserted by Max Weber – will influence the mode of people's economic behaviour. In fact Pareto regarded socialism as a kind of religion; he believed that, just as the appearance of Protestantism had influenced people's ethos and work ethics, so socialism changed people's motivations, altering the economic system they supported.[2]

IV

I now want to try and change, and adjust the terminology used up to now. Since what I have thus far called 'broad economics' deals with questions usually regarded as being dealt with by economics, I will from here on simply call it 'economics'. By contrast what I have been calling 'economics in the much wider sense', I will henceforward call 'comprehensive economics', since it looks at things connected with economics, including problems that are not normally dealt with in economics. I shall refer to 'economics in the narrow sense' just as 'economics theory'.

If we use this kind of vocabulary, it is possible to make the following statement. In normal 'economics' economic actions in both the broad and the narrow sense are dealt with together, while in standard 'economic theory' – for example the theories of scholars such as Walras and Hicks, and even more so postwar economists such as Debreu and Hahn – economic actions in the broad sense are tacitly ignored. Only economic actions in the narrow sense are analysed, all others being assumed not to exist. For those persons who neglect economic actions in the broader sense, 'economics' and 'economic theory' become one and the same, and we end up with economics as the study of routine, logical economic actions.

Non-routine economic actions are outside the routine application of logical economic laws. The significance of these kinds of action was emphasised by Schumpeter. His view was that entrepreneurs are far from being normal individuals who act in a textbook fashion driven by calculations of profit and utility. Only unusual individuals of the entrepreneur type can become entrepreneurs. This requires special characteristics; their decisions are individualistic, not governed by principles which can be laid *a priori*. Moreover, such individuals have to be possessed of greater leadership qualities than others. The actions of this kind of entrepreneur are not those of a human type which establishes 'principles of entrepreneur behaviour' and then follows the course of action logically dictated by those principles. These kinds of individual must have, as their requisites, abilities to understand people's sentiments and to appeal to their feelings, in addition to the passion which will sway them. Since they act on the basis of apparently original ideas, entrepreneurial activity cannot be analysed merely through utility analysis or marginal productivity analysis. In extreme cases entrepreneurs are people who feel they have a mission just to find out whether or not the innovation they have thought of is actually workable, and whether it can become highly successful work. The result is that these entrepreneurs do not carry on their work with the objective of making a profit, which means that when it becomes clear that their businesses are firmly on the right lines and able to make a profit, they lose interest in these businesses, selling them off and moving to new enterprises. There are many of these fickle entrepreneurs. It can even be said that it is this very kind of person who is the entrepreneur among entrepreneurs – the pure entrepreneur. This fact is well demonstrated by the fact that a country which has effected a great many innovations is not necessarily blessed with economic success. Just look at the case of Britain. A theory of entrepreneurs requires an understanding of the entrepreneurial spirit, and for that reason requires us to provide ourselves with a certain kind of theory of non-logical behaviour.

V

Another kind of non-routine economic activity can be found in the take-over. In Tobin's q-ratio theory we have a logical theory which uses profit calculation to explain in what kind of circumstances takeovers will occur. As is well known, the q ratio is derived by estimating the market value of the net assets possessed by the enterprise and dividing the total share value of the enterprise (its total market value) by this sum. If $q < 1$ the total share value of the enterprise is less than the value of the net assets, so if the enterprise is taken over through buying up shares the net assets obtained will be in excess of the cost needed to do this, and the enterprise's takeover will achieve a profit. Thus where $q < 1$ the enterprise will be taken over, while if $q > 1$ the enterprise will be safe.

At first glance this would appear a rational theory to which we can have few objections, but if we look at the actual economy we find that the size of q has little to do with whether or not enterprises are the object of a take-over. There are many enterprises which are not taken over where $q < 1$, and others where there is a takeover although $q > 1$.

In the latter case, therefore, why is it that the takeover is carried out in full knowledge that a direct loss will be incurred thereby? Let us suppose, for example, that there are two competing enterprises, A and B. Let us assume $q_B > 1$, whilst it is immaterial whether q_A is greater or lesser than 1. If we now assume that A takes over B, just by doing so it will incur a loss. However, if it eventually eliminates B, A's position will be enhanced because one of its competitors will have gone. The aim of obtaining this kind of indirect benefit can be enough to make A initiate a takeover. Nevertheless, this indirect benefit is not certain, and the takeover is not necessarily carried out even if the benefit is great. Behind such an action there is likely to bc the animosity and fear which A feels towards B. As long as we fail to explain sufficiently this kind of sentiment, the q theory of takeovers will be little but a fabrication. If we understand non-illogical modes of activity, it would be accepted as very reasonable that enterprise A, which is aware of the danger that it will be the object of a takeover as $q_A < 1$, may make a pre-emptive attack and take over B. In short, there does not exist any purely logical economic theory relating to who initiates a takeover, and under what circumstances.

Let me give one more example. In West Germany in 1976 it was decided that in all companies with more than 2000 employees the shareholders' meeting would select a certain number of *Aufsichtsrat*, who would constitute a committee along with the same number of *Aufsichtsrat* chosen by the employee side, and that committee would make decisions concerning important management problems. This practice marked a considerable concession on the part of the shareholders, but there is no purely economic logic behind their having to make such a concession. Why should the employee representatives share *Aufsichtsrat* with those of shareholders in the very proportions of fifty-fifty? It only resulted from the shareholders being compelled to acknowledge an equivalent social power on the part of the employees. It is not possible to discuss this kind of problem in terms of the conventional, axiomatic economics, and even if we consider this as the establishment of some sort of balance of power by means of a kind of game between shareholders and employees, the game's pay-off matrix is not defined, so it cannot be explained in game-theoretic terms. This kind of problem is a problem of economics outside what I have called 'narrow economics'.

Now we cannot make any *a priori* assertion as to the likely results of non-logical activity. We have no choice but to observe a large number of examples – and though it may be non-routine activity, there exist a great enough number of such instances – and to observe with great care the kinds of result that occur. With the results obtained in this manner, the theoretical model is constructed inductively.

Where the theoretical conclusions thus deduced from this kind of model do not accord with the state of affairs that exists in the real economy, the model is refuted and has to be reconstructed into a more appropriate one. Thus the element of 'broad economics' in 'economics' is methodologically inductive and empirical, and has a totally contrasting character to the elements of 'narrow economic theory', which are axiomatic, deductive and mathematical. Schumpeter's economics is regarded as being impossible to formulate analytically, and this can be said to stem from this kind of situation.

VI

It has been suggested above that there is a strong similarity between Schumpeter and Pareto, whether or not Schumpeter himself was aware of it. For a start, Schumpeter developed an analysis of economic activity which belongs outside the sphere of economic activity based on standard utility or profit calculation. Pareto showed a keen interest in the analysis of this kind of non-logical activity. He produced a huge volume of general analytical rules, but was almost totally unable to point out relevant major problems and give them a theoretical explanation. In that sense it can be said that the examples of Pareto's analysis of non-logical economic activity are empty, or something pretty close to it. By contrast, while Schumpeter failed to achieve a complete analysis, and his examples hardly rested on a profound methodology, he did highlight the existence of some very important examples of this kind. One of these is his theory of innovation. By doing this, he filled Pareto's empty box with a range of subject matters.

Secondly, Schumpeter presented his famous – and totally anti-Marxian – theory of system transformation, or theory of revolution;[3] this kind of theory can be seen as an application of Pareto's theories relating to the rise and decline of the ruling class – the rise and fall of élites. More will be said in detail on this point later on. Unlike Marx's theory of system transformation, which is based on a theory of class conflict, these other theories of transformation are based on the existence of hegemonic struggle within the ruling class. It is appropriate to call Pareto's whole system, which brings together this kind of anti-Marxian social theory with orthodox economics, a neoclassical comprehension, but it was Schumpeter who can be seen as the heir of this grand design of Pareto's.

Pareto's comprehensive economics imply refutation or at least a revision of the materialist view of history. In this, Pareto's sociology – his theories of social equilibrium and dynamics – plays an important role. In Marx, as well, we find a magnificent synthesised economics which includes an analysis of the superstructure, but because the study of the superstructure is, as it were, detached from its own economics, this economics, in the narrow sense of the word, is no different from normal economics (for example, neoclassical theory) in that it consistently remains the study of logical activity. By contrast, in the case of Pareto's integrated economics no such separation can be made, so we end up with a structure where, strictly speaking, it is not possible to abstract from it a self-contained, normal economics, i.e. the study of logical activity.

Pareto's comprehensive economics is thus multidisciplinary. At the same time, as we have already seen, the methodology is not a unitary one. First of all the section on general economic equilibrium theory which deals with logical activity is 'geometrically constructed' exactly in the manner of Spinoza, as shown later in the Arrow-Debreu and Arrow-Hahn theories which perfected it. This theory is a purely deductive inference of the implication of axiomatically formulated economic principles. By contrast, for non-logical actions there are no such principles, and we have no alternative but to discover the rules inductively and empirically. The task of explaining in a logically convincing way why the results of non-logical actions of this kind are as they are, falls to the non-geometric part of the integrated economics.

VII

Let us look at this in a bit more detail. Pareto prepared his main work on sociology, *Trattato di sociologia generale*, with a view to analysing people's non-logical behaviour.[4] He believed that instinct, emotion or feelings were the predominant forces in determining non-logical behaviour, and called these the residues. He studied inductively what kinds of residue existed. However, just pointing out what kinds of residue exist is not in itself a convincing explanation of actions based on those residues. Pareto termed the reasonings for why a certain residue stimulates a particular course of action, or the arguments justifying these kinds of reasonings, 'derivations'. A derivation is an attempt to give a logical explanation to a non-logical action; as people's capacity for logical thought develops, so what could have been a derivation at one stage of development ceases to be able to play the role of a derivation at a subsequent stage. For that research new derivations are sought. Just as religion has become gradually more rational with the advances of human knowledge and society, so too have religious derivations evolved and developed. Derivations are thus a product of history, and constantly changing. The resultants brought about by residues and derivations were termed by Pareto 'derivatives'. This demonstrates our recognition of non-logical behaviour.

This kind of theory of non-logical behaviour consists of two elements: one which is an inductive observation of residues, and the other an element of deductive reasoning, which must be both quasi-logical as historical fact, and perfectly logical as an ideal and complete derivation. Pareto's sociology is therefore the methodological antithesis of pure economics. The former is inductive-logical, while the inductive element in the latter is zero or negligible, rendering it purely or mainly deductive (or axiomatic). As has already been suggested, economics will increasingly in the future have to research non-logical behaviour as well, and this branch of research will need to devise laws inductively and explain them rationally. Thus it is not just comprehensive economics but economics as well which will be a methodological hybrid – empirical, inductive, logical and deductive.

VIII

Now if the relationship between these two elements – the empirical-deductive and the transcendental-logical – is a separable, one-sided one, as is the case in Marxian theory, the methodological structure of the comprehensive economics can be succinctly stated. In the case of Pareto, however, there is no such separation, but a relation of mutual influence. To elaborate on this, in Marxian theory, the parts for which we need empirical, inductive analysis – namely the areas of political structure, legal system, learning and culture, and the structure of human knowledge and consciousness (the so-called superstructure) – are determined by the nature of the substructure, i.e. the relations of production which are in turn determined by productive forces. Marx took the view that the reverse relationship, namely the superstructure influencing the substructure either does not exist at all, or is negligible. Any study of the superstructure is therefore a derivation of the study of the basic structure, that is, economics. For that reason economics for Marx clarified the fundamental movements of society, and played the commanding role among the various social sciences.

Pareto's broader economics, with its assumptions of a mutually interactive relationship between the superstructure and the substructure, is not just more logically universal than Marx's theory with its assumption of a one-sided relationship between the two, but also more realistic. This is abundantly apparent if we take a close look at a wide range of past history, as Pareto himself did. The very question of whether the relationship between the two is one-sided or two-sided needs an inductive, empirical judgement. If Pareto was right on this point – and I believe that he was – then both the neoclassical theorists with their attempts to structure economics axiomatically and the Marxian economists with their purely economic explanations of social trends are totally mistaken. Such explanations must be at the very least extremely one-sided and imperfect. Pareto did not necessarily succeed in synthesising sociology and economics, but it is not difficult to identify in his work a declared intention of reaching such a synthesis, and the outline for doing so. My own belief is that it was Schumpeter who advanced economics a considerable way down the road intended by Pareto.

IX

Pareto indicated the following six residues – instinct for combinations, instinct for group-persistence, tendency to express any strong emotion by external action, residues of sociability, residues of concerning the integrity of the individual, and the sex residue. It is the first two of these which can be regarded as being of theoretical importance, and therefore in need of some explanation.

As the translators of the *Trattato* into English stated in the translation, the Italian word 'combinazione' was translated into English as 'combination', even though they were unhappy with this. According to them the Italian word 'combination' embraced a much broader meaning than the English one, with the phrase 'the instinct for combination suggesting "the inventive faculty", "ingeniousness", "originality", "imagination" and so on'.[5] In fact, as Pareto, too, stated in explaining combinational activities, 'The scientist in his laboratory makes combinations according to certain norms, certain purposes, certain hypotheses, for the most part rational (at times he combines at random).'[6] Now all kinds of innovation are the fruits of activities of this nature, so the 'instinct for combinations' could probably be translated as 'the instinct for innovation'. It is true, as Pareto himself commented, that 'The ignorant person makes combinations in view of analogies that are mostly fantastic, absurd, childish (often also by chance).'[7] Such being frequently the case, positive results of course cannot be obtained from these. Whatever the case, attempts to obtain results from combinational activities are non-logical acts, whether or not the attempts are successful.

Interpreted in this way it is clear that Pareto's *combinazione* residue and Schumpeter's theory of innovation are closely related to each other. Individuals possessing this kind of residue are progressive and innovative; entrepreneurs can be seen as the embodiment of this special type of person. Schumpeter took the view that because capitalist society was one dominated by entrepreneurs, capitalism, or the free enterprise system, was of itself innovatory. Socialist society was regarded as one where this instinct had become paralysed. After around 1903, when *Les Systèmes socialistes* was published, Pareto reached a more positive evaluation of socialism.

Human behaviour, he believed, consisted of that based on logically conceived doctrines and that based on non-logical passions and feelings. A socialist movement based on socialist doctrines fell into the former category, but this was not simply logical behaviour; it was accompanied by non-logical behaviour – that based on an 'instinct for combination' which gave people the will-power to try and contribute to the making of a new and better society, and stirred up in them fierce passions. Pareto emphasised the latter aspect and considered that what was important for socialism was not the theory, but the passion to push forward the doctrine. Marxian theory might have its deficiencies – and Pareto believed that it did – and its theory of value might be wrong, but such things have had little impact on socialism. 'All this has hurt the socialist faith little or not at all. It was not the book by Marx which has created socialists; it is the socialists who have made Marx's book famous'.[8] The 'new and better society' may be nothing more than a myth, a mere castle in the air. Even so, Pareto adjudged it to be a powerful factor in mobilising the masses. Such passions gave an energy to the mass of people and enabled them to realise their aspirations. Liberalism might appeal to their reason, but socialism mobilised their feelings. Liberalism held no appeal to the feelings of the masses, however much it might stir up the passion of the intelligentsia. (This cannot, perhaps, be said of the present time, but Pareto's conclusion was almost certainly correct at the start of the twentieth century.) Thus socialist activity was politically that much more effective than liberal activity, causing Pareto to evaluate socialism positively.

Pareto believed that socialism could achieve the same things as could a market economy. His *Manuele d'economia politica* was published in 1906, with a revised edition in French, *Manuel d'économie politique* appearing in 1909. In these works, as in E. Barone's work 'Il Ministro della produzione nello stato collettivista' (*Giornale degli economisti*) published in 1908, it was recognised that a socialist society could work in exactly the same way as a society based on private ownership in perfectly competitive conditions. Pareto is said to have told Schumpeter that he was himself a socialist[9] and it is undoubtedly true that, at least at certain times, Pareto's evaluation of socialism was more positive than that of Schumpeter.

X

Pareto's second items, the residues of group persistences or residues of persistence of aggregates (class II residues), are the antithesis of the residues of combination which have just been described (class I residues). While these latter reflect the spirit of enterprise of the individual, the former reflect the spirit of service. Using these two kinds of residue, Pareto discussed the changes in society which might be brought about by a policy of industrial protection; the example of protectionism which he took is not appropriate for the contemporary world, but a good modern example would probably be anti-socialist policies, starting with Thatcher's privatisation policy. Needless to say this kind of policy is aimed at promoting the spirit of capitalism, and those individuals who are well endowed with class I residues, while their class II residues are not plentiful, are likely under the policy to take a larger share in the upper levels of society. The country will thereby be stimulated in the direction of economic pursuits and industrialism.[10]

However, the country will not progress for ever in this same direction. Eventually there will be a movement in the opposite direction; there will come a time when power is held by the type of individuals who are rich in the residues of group-persistence, who will not give pride of place to their own individual economic gain (that is, the socialist-type). The upper levels of society will be taken over by a different type of person. The élites are thus circulating.

The fact that a society which has hitherto been progressing in one direction then switches to head in another direction is, according to Pareto, not the result of an automatic change, but invariably the result of war, 'as was the case in the conquest of Greece by Rome, Greece at the time possessing class I residues of very great abundance, while in Rome the advantage lay with the residues of group persistence (class II)'.[11] Moreover, he recognised that revolutions and major political changes brought about major changes in the proportions of residues in the ruling class. Whatever the case, though, Pareto regarded external factors such as war and revolution as provoking social change.

Schumpeter's transformation of society did not necessitate this kind of exogenous factor. Once industrialisation had progressed beyond a certain point, other factors did not necessarily appear, but it was seen as inevitably giving rise to socialisation. That is to say, in Schumpeter's case social change was spontaneous. It was those spontaneous changes which were democratic, obviating the need for violence.

It is true that when Schumpeter devised his theory he gave fair consideration to Pareto's ideas. In fact, as we shall see below, there can be regarded as being a close connection between Pareto's theory of the circulation of élites and Schumpeter's theory of the transformation from capitalism to socialism. In the part of his work entitled 'Can Capitalism Survive?' Schumpeter refers to Pareto's *'circulation des aristocraties'*[12], and in the chapter discussing 'The Human Element' he acknowledges Pareto's *Trattato* (The Mind and Society) as representing a way of thinking concerning human nature in the latter half of the nineteenth century.[13] Despite this, however, Schumpeter used none of Pareto's analytical tools, apart from mentioning Pareto's *circulation des aristocraties*.[14] Schumpeter is for this reason normally talked about quite separately from Pareto. I believe, however, that there is a strong connection between the two, in fact Schumpeter can even be regarded as a revised version or modification of Pareto. To use Pareto's words, Schumpeter's entrepreneurs are individuals with plentiful residues of combination, while socialists are the type of people with more of the residues of group-persistence. Now as industrialisation advance there is a gradual decrease in investment opportunities in the sphere of industry, and industry ceases to be an attractive place for individuals with strong residues of combination to work in. Moreover, because even those who do not have considerable residues of combination can carry through industrial innovations by creating committees and working together, the degree of separation between residues of combination and industry increases. In contrast to this, in social welfare and other areas upon which we have hitherto turned our backs, the possibility of discovering new combinations increases, and the residues of combination and the residues of group persistence become complimentary rather than conflicting. Thus intellectual concern comes to focus on the challenging new work of making innovations in the areas of relief for the poor and social welfare; the capitalist system ceases to be able to impede this new trend, and eventually the system is metamorphosed into socialism. For such a metamorphosis to occur does not require the external stimulus of war or revolution. The structures are transformed of themselves; no other force is needed.

XI

The sociological methodology developed by Pareto was a grandiose one, but he made relatively little use of it to carry out any theoretical or concrete examination of problems in sociology and economics. The only exception to this is the discussion of the theory of circulation of élites and social equilibrium in history found in volume IV of the *Trattato*. (And I think that this is the reason why his sociology failed to find any popularity particularly amongst us, economists.) In contrast to this, Schumpeter managed a

splendid discussion of those issues relating to what I have called economics in the broad sense of the word, but his methodological standpoint is not
the most lucid. There are, of course, errors in his theory, especially when
seen from a present which has witnessed the collapse of the socialist states
of the Soviet Union and Eastern Europe, and modifications are for that reason necessary.

Schumpeter does not, for example, discuss the kind of socialist exploitation[15] which Catephores and I have looked at. In fact the Soviet Union and
the countries of Eastern Europe developed to a sufficiently high degree for
socialist exploitation to be intolerable, and the collapse occurred because
this was closely tied to socialist autocracy. Schumpeter's acknowledge-
ment of socialist autocracy[16] was, it must be said, somewhat indulgent, at
least when seen from the perspective of today. Moreover, the inefficiency
of socialist bureaucracy (a major factor in the socialist exploitation of
Morishima-Catephores) should also be regarded as more important.

Even more fundamentally, Schumpeter's vision was that as time passes,
divisions appear within the capitalist camp, so the more progressive elements will throw in their lot with labour. However, the opposite must be
regarded as equally important, namely a division within the labour camp,
with its more conservative elements joining the capitalist side, such as we
saw in Britain in the 1980s and afterwards. If we take this perspective, it is
still possible to extract many features of the 'broad economics' from
Pareto's *Trattato*.

XII

Finally, let me say something simply about the way in which this book has
been edited. The text itself is a personal revamping of the works of Alfonso
de Pietri-Tonelli and G.H. Bousquet, both of whom were authorities on
Pareto. On the tenth anniversary of Pareto's death de Pietri-Tonelli gave an
address to the Economic Section of the Italian Association for the Advancement of Science, the text of which was published in the *Revista di politica
economia*, December 1934 and January 1935, under the title 'Vilfredo
Pareto (15 Iuglio 1848 – 19 Agosto 1923)'. The first and second chapters of
the present work contain the first half of this address, namely the part which
gave a brief biography of Pareto and discussed him as an economist. When
discussing Pareto's achievements as an economist, it is, of course, impossible to disregard his contribution to general equilibrium theory, but to do
this would need more space than is available. To make up for this lack in

the present volume, I have put in as Chapter 3 de Pietri-Tonelli's 'Le equazioni generali dell' equilibrio economico di Vilfredo Pareto', published in the *Revista di politica economia*, although I do not necessarily regard it as entirely suitable and of high quality. In contrast to these, Chapters 4, 5, 6 and 7 look at Pareto as a sociologist. The first three of these are translations of chapters 4, 5, 6 of the work of G.H. Bousquet, *Vilfredo Pareto, sa vie et son oeuvre* (Paris: Payot, 1928). Chapter 7 continues again with the address by de Pietri-Tonelli. Pareto was a reflection of the turbulent conditions of his time, associated with many ideologies – liberalism, socialism, fascism. If one were to speak well of him, he would have the wide range of interests appropriate to a social scientist; if badly, he could be viewed as intellectually fickle: to put it bluntly, a man lacking intellectual integrity. What needs to be made particularly clear is his relationship with fascism, and Pareto himself, I think, would have wanted that. Both Bousquet, in the latter half of Chapter 6, and de Pietri-Tonelli, in Chapter 7, discuss whether or not Pareto himself was a fascist, but the answer to the question seems essentially to rest with the views of the respondent, so it must be regarded as a matter of importance to record the independent opinions of these two writers.

In a review of the collection of Pareto's letters to Pantaleoni,[17] Hicks asks: 'how did it [Pareto's economics] sit, in Pareto's mind, with these other things [such as political views on Fascism, etc.] that seem so much less acceptable?' This is closely related to the problem of *Wertfreiheit* (freedom from value judgements) posed and discussed by Max Weber and others, as Hicks himself puts the matter in the following very Hicksian manner. 'Human relations between the scientist and his material are a weakness. Sympathy is therefore a weakness; but if sympathy is a weakness, antipathy is also.' One may consider that only a 'strong' man who is free from these weaknesses is suited for working in the areas of social sciences where the observations of the facts may conspicously be affected and distorted by the scientist's ideology or his philosophy of life, as they may be very much so in the 'comprehensive' economics. There is, however, an inevitable dilemma that such a strong man, who frees himself from all sorts of value judgements and is, therefore, indifferent and impartial in matters connected with ideologies, would be uninterested in the academic work in such areas of social sciences. I think that for a social scientist to overcome this dilemma, it would be no use his making efforts to cleanse himself from all kinds of conscious or hidden ideologies. His academic interest would unavoidably be biased because of his *Weltanschauung* or philosophy of life, even his logical derivations of conclusions, could be contaminated with his (unconscious) wishful reasoning. However, an accumulation of even such works over a long period will eventually enable us to find the part of the comprehensive economics which remains to be invariant with respect to the scientists' value judgements.

Chapter 8, also, comes from de Pietri-Tonelli's address. In it he discusses the development of economics in the ten years following Pareto's death and discusses in that context the achievements of Pareto. Those ten years had witnessed an extraordinary development in economics, and a 'modernisation' of the discipline. By the end of this period the Econometric Society had been founded and the publication of *Econometrica* had begun, and the progress of Anglo-American economists was conspicuous. I believe that this period was one of exceptional importance, and it is a source of regret to me that the postwar world of economics, particularly nowadays, does not attach any great importance to the recollection of these years. It is in that sense that it is of value to have such a record in English, though even that is far from being sufficient.

MICHIO MORISHIMA

Abbreviations

The following abbreviations are used in references throughout the text to the works of Pareto and of Georges Bousquet.

C   *Le Cours d'économie politique*
Ss   *Les Systèmes socialistes*
M   *Le Manuel d'économie politique*
S   *Le Traite de sociologie generale* (Trattato di sociologia generale)
F   *Fatti e teorie*
T   *Trasformazione*

Is   *Introduction aux systèmes de Pareto* (Bousquet)
P   *Précis de systèmes d'après V. Pareto* (Bousquet)

1 A Short Biography

Alfonso de Pietri-Tonelli

Vilfredo Pareto's scientific and philosophical personality was both wide-ranging and adventurous. His knowledge of the more complex branches of contemporary mathematics and physics was considerable and he possessed an insatiable thirst for knowledge indicative of his vocation for speculative thought. Though his professional life was long, his participation in politics was occasional and took place almost exclusively through the written word. His family life was not very happy and he dedicated himself totally to study. He remained aloof from the academic politics which often poison a scientist's life, and the distracting quarrels over money which are of little value as practical economic experience. During his lifetime he avoided the type of politics which instils blind ambition for power in the mind of the scholar, at the expense of the noble thirst for knowledge; with this type of politics, usually what is lost to science is not gained in political service to the country.

Pareto's twenty years of teaching from a chair which became famous all over the world[1] were tiring due to a severe illness. He undertook an enormous amount of work in different fields: two very different treatises on economics, a critique of socialist systems and a critique of virtuosity, a major treatise on general sociology, numerous articles on economics, mathematical statistics, political criticism and sociology, besides numerous economic and political critiques published both in Italian and foreign journals, and unforgettable contributions to several fields such as mathematics, statistics, economics, politics and sociology. His chief merit lies, however, in having contributed to the transformation of economics and in part also sociology, from a mainly pre-scientific into a largely scientific discipline.

During his lifetime, his schools of thought on economics and sociology were unrivalled in Italy and have since attracted a growing number of students of his works. Most of these students are continuing his work, some attempting new approaches. Ten years after the death of Pareto, his fame continues to spread, while writers and theoreticians who once held sway have fallen into oblivion. Our aim here is to illustrate systematically Pareto's contribution as a theoretician, so as to critically assess the great thinker from Céligny during both his own lifetime and ours. He will be considered as a theoretician, that is, as an economist and a statistician, as a sociologist and political scientist, but above all as a scientist and practical inspirer of specific

1

economic and political movements. We will also examine his theories and
their current and potential value.

* * *

Pareto's father came from an old noble family in Genoa and although his
mother was French, Pareto's character and feelings were Italian. He [was
born in 1848, and] spent the first years of his life in Paris where his father
was in exile. On returning to Italy [in 1858], he [later] studied technical
subjects and engineering. His profession took him to Florence and
subsequently to Fiesole. During his years in industry he dedicated himself to
the study of the classics, science and social studies. He was attracted to the
problems raised by economic policy and turned principally to the study of
classical economic theory of which he recognised himself as a follower. He
became familiar with these theories through the 'Economist's Library'
which was famous as a result of its direction by Francesco Ferrara. His early
studies in mathematical economics had made him well-known and well
thought of and subsequently he was called, in his intellectual and physical
prime, to succeed Walras to the chair in Lausanne where he 'learned by
teaching'. This was the road which led him to his peaceful retreat in Céligny
where he spent many hours totally engrossed in methodical study. His
activities as a student of economic and social life, which during his lifetime
caused him to tower over others, took place in the last quarter of the
nineteenth century and the first quarter of the twentieth. This was a period of
the great economic and social changes which culminated in the First World
War. An initial period of decline was followed by expansion and great economic prosperity, then came inflation and finally deflation. Great political
change took place in this period, with the fall of liberalism and the rise of
parliamentary democracy, socialism, trade unionism, interventionism,
Communism, Fascism and nationalism. Great technical and practical
changes were made possible by the development of the physical sciences
based on the solid foundation of mathematical theory, observation and
experimentation. The study of the social sciences was greatly intensified and
the dominion of science over philosophy was established.

* * *

Chronologically over less than thirty years Pareto's works were:

Cours d'économie politique, Lausanne, volume I, 1896, volume II, 1897;

Les Systèmes socialistes, Paris, volumes I and II, 1903 (reprint 1926); *Manuale di economia politica*, Milan, 1906 (reprint 1919), translated into French with a new appendix: *Manuel d'économie politique*, Paris, 1909 (reprint 1927); 'Economie mathématique', in *Encyclopédie des sciences mathématiques* section I, volume IV, part 4, Paris, 1911; *Le Mythe vertuiste et la littérature immorale*, Paris, 1911; the second (Italian) edition: *Il mito virtuista e la letteratura immorale*, Rome, 1914, was expanded by the author.

Trattato di sociologia generale, Florence, volumes I and II, 1916, French translation: *Traité de sociologie générale*, Lausanne, 1919, second Italian edition with additions, Florence, volumes I, II and III, 1923; *Fatti e teorie*, Florence, 1920; *Trasformazione della democrazia*, Milan, 1921.

The ideas that were to be developed in his work can be seen early on in the speech which the 'Marquis Vilfredo Pareto, ordinary member' made at a public meeting held by the Royal Academy of the Georgofili, on 29 April 1877, entitled 'the logic of the new schools of economics'. The general president of the academy had the speech 'published in the press urging the readers to study the subject and let the academy know the results of these studies'. This speech, which is one of the earliest records of Pareto's ideas, was found with the author's dedication in a school copybook in Ferrara's library which is kept at ca'Foscari [Venice].

We have listed only the most substantial works, whose content is familiar to everyone. These writings are, however, preceded, accompanied and followed by lesser works which are complementary so that as regards Pareto, his writings should be judged less by their volume than in the case of other writers.

Pareto was continually reconsidering the difficult problems which he had posed himself in his obsessive research, so as to simplify formulations and find easier solutions. Ever dissatisfied, he kept returning to problems, examining them from another point of view, in order to further his investigation without nullifying what he had already written. It was as if he were too busy working and reworking to have time to summarise and order; his references to his earlier ideas were implicit rather than explicit, he referred back rather than giving a resumé of his earlier work. Thus it is necessary to look for his thoughts on particular subjects in various works which complement each other. Although minor works are always useful, in this case they are essential for a better understanding of the major ones.

The articles which precede Pareto's more important works, those for example which appeared in the *Giornale degli economisti* in its heyday, all belong to the exacting preparatory stage of the work. They were written before the *Cours*, the *Manuale* and the *Manuel* and include the articles which appeared in the *Rivista italiana di sociologia* prior to the *Trattato*. They illustrate the formative stages of the author's theories which were often based on the paradigms of the physical or other sciences that Pareto always kept in mind. They show us the projects he followed up and those he rejected later and the gestation of his thought which could provide the elements for an interesting chapter on the psychology of scientific endeavour.

The articles which accompany or follow the basic works help to develop and apply the theories, thus clarifying and reinforcing them. We can cite the example in economics of the contribution to the *Encyclopédie des sciences mathématiques*, and in sociology the epilogue to *Fatti e teorie* and the article on the *Trasformazione della democrazia*, in particular its appendix.

Pareto also wrote articles dealing with specific subjects which consequently are valuable in themselves, such as the articles on interpolation.

Just as the size of the book has only a relative importance in Pareto, so also his titles do not always reflect the content. A superficial reader who does not concentrate on the argument in scientific writings (which are not written like practical manuals) may find the distribution of the contents between the text and the notes disorganised. Furthermore he may note that what amounts to preparatory drafts of basic works are to be found not only in various articles but also in chapters of previous works dealing with other subjects. This is true especially of the *Trattato*, the first lines of which are to be found in different parts of the *Cours*, the *Manuale* and the *Manuel*, as well as in articles and volumes such as *Systèmes socialistes* and *Mythe vertuiste* and *Mito virtuista*.

Theory in Pareto's writings is developed in different parts of the same work and from one work to another. Pareto dealt with vast and varied subjects in his work, and its content requires reorganisation, along the lines of the theories. Thus, today, thirty-eight years after the publication of the *Cours*, [1896], twenty-eight after the publication of the *Manuale* and eighteen after the *Trattato*, the complex personality of Vilfredo Pareto is revealed. In order to make a rigorous critical judgement, we must analyse and synthesise the various and complementary aspects of his work, without distinguishing principal from secondary ones.

For this reason we shall look at Pareto first as an economist and subsequently as a statistician, a sociologist and a political scientist; finally we will consider Vilfredo Pareto as principally a scientist.

2 The Economist

Alfonso de Pietri-Tonelli

Pareto writes as an economist in most of the *Cours*, in the *Manuale*, especially in its appendix, in the appendix of the *Manuel*, in the article in the *Encyclopédie des sciences mathématiques* and the articles which came before and after these works.

It is not true that there are no schools of economics or that there are only two, as Pantaleoni argued in one of his sensational and paradoxical declarations.

In economics, as in all the other sciences, be they social, biological or physical, there always were, are and will be different schools of thought. It would be useless to deny it. In economics also, these different schools have their recognised leaders. Often they are so distinct from one another in the content and form of their respective doctrines that the disciples of one find it difficult to understand the disciples of another. This is true of the literary economists, who do not or can not understand, much less judge, the mathematical economists.

Likewise, scientific groups are basically social groups and thus their essential characteristics are shared by economic groups for these too are in essence social groups. Thus any theory about such groups will be a specific chapter in a general theory of social groups.

The diversity in schools of thought in economics also derive from differences and peculiarities in philosophical points of view, in methods of investigation, intentions and forms of exposition. From the start two groups of schools of economic thought can be distinguished (as we shall later distinguish, in general, two groups of scientific thought) but we shall deal only with the first group. We shall differentiate those economic schools of thought that use the least imperfect scientific methods, in order better to capture the reality of the economy. These are directly linked to the different phases of development of the logical tools of science and form part of the general scientific movement of our age. Those schools of economics which are extraneous to this development and do not use current scientific tools, have no place in the history of science but belong to the history of such fields as philosophy, literature, politics, etc., and must be differentiated from the above schools of thought.

Pareto wrote of methods, which are often considered the fundamental distinguishing factor, that are all correct in economics (and not only in economics, it may be added) as long as they lead to a theory which represents reality, if that is the aim. Moreover, in specific cases, it is not necessary to proceed from action to theory. We can construct a theory and then proceed to provide evidence and test it. The important thing is that it should correspond to reality. Certainly intuition reigns sovereign in the world of thought as well as in that of action. It depends on vocation and gathers force from external circumstances which can be appropriate but are sometimes casual, even insignificant events. Experiment and observation are usually relegated to the more modest but no less important function of controlling the value of the original inspiration. The progress of science, like that of action, is always long and arduous and sometimes ideas or institutions can be arrived at in surprising ways from beginnings which seemed to point to opposite conclusions.

Pareto used various methods without excluding any on principle. He observed the present and reconstructed the past, by helping with the editing of a 'Library of economic history' in Italy. He made use of statistics, ordinary reasoning or mathematical analysis as was necessary, convenient or fruitful. He used any means of investigation as long as it formed part of what he defined generically as the logical-experimental method of observation. He excelled, however, in the use of the least imperfect scientific method, the quantitative mathematical method tested by the observation of reality.

Two phases can be distinguished in the use of this method in Pareto's research into economics. The first phase culminates in the theories of the *Cours*, the second in the theories of the *Manuale*, the appendix to the *Manuel* and in the articles in the *Encyclopédie des sciences mathématiques*.

The *Cours* is the first substantial work Pareto produced and was published when he was forty-eight. It is a collection of the lectures he gave at the University of Lausanne and also includes previous writings linked to the theories elaborated in the *Cours*. Pareto begins by developing one of Walras's brilliant ideas to which his attention had been drawn in the *Principi di economia pura* by Pantaleoni's suggestions. The latter was unable to make full use of Walras's analytical procedure due to his lack of knowledge of the necessary mathematics. Although initially he was side-tracked by metaphysical digressions on the theory of the social ideal, the influence of Cournot's analysis, which had inspired Walras himself to apply infinitesimal mathematics to economics, prevailed along with that of Jevons, Edgeworth, Fisher and Marshall. Pareto always kept in mind the theories of the classical economists as Ferrara had presented them. He elaborated the theories of economic equilibrium, determining its conditions by using a logical procedure based on that used in mechanics in similar cases. In the *Cours* he considers the cases of trade and production, of capitalisation, of money, of international trade with free competition, monopoly, and state socialism. He deals with most of the arguments on the basis of principles which are covered in ordinary economics textbooks and although his order of exposition is innovative, it is not excessively so. There is greater balance between the different parts of this book than in his subsequent works which, although more original, are rather hurried in parts. The *Cours* brings formal rigour to the classical theories of population, monetary systems, the banks, income and wages, extending them and correcting any errors.

Moreover his use of mathematics goes well beyond that of any of his predecessors. Thus he brings greater analytical rigour to the notion of economic utility, taken as a complex function and calls it 'ophelimity'[1] to avoid ambiguity of terminology. His systems of equilibrium equations have quite different unknowns from those considered by Walras (the quantities exchanged by individual traders) and he analyses the variable and measurable coefficients of production mathematically, developing one of Walras's ideas. He considers the maximum ophelimity for a collectivity, the real movements of population as the result of innumerable circumstances and the virtual movements determined by generative forces. He formulates mathematically and generalises Ricardo's theory of income. He deals with speculation on the stock exchange, defining its nature and considering its conditions (competition and monopoly). He deals with coalitions. He offers a theory of economic fluctuations. He progresses gradually from pure to applied economics, approaching economic reality by means of a consideration of economic systems and the study of distribution and consumption.

His approach is completely different, in the *Manuale* and the appendix of the *Manuel*, and in those writings linked to the theories expounded in these two texts. It seems to be the work of another author from that of the *Cours*. Pareto seems to enjoy himself in the *Manuale*, treating the author of the *Cours* as if he were a different person. He criticises and recognises the errors in his own point of view, the theories under consideration and the organisation of the subject matter. Not many people would dare to make such criticisms of the *Cours*; and they are of a kind that authors usually make of the work of others, most authors being far more indulgent towards their own. Despite his criticisms, Pareto often refers to the theories in the *Cours* that he did not wish to discard. He had thought of writing a second edition which would have been completely new in parts and a third volume which would have dealt with mathematical economics, without the constraints of teaching needs or space. The well-known appendix of the *Manuel* is a summary of this. Maybe this project, which he aired continually but never completed, was behind his refusal to let the *Cours* be reprinted, despite our request for him to do so. It is deplorable that the *Cours* should not be reprinted since a new edition is out of the question. It has been out of print for two years and has become the subject of speculation by antiquarian book-dealers whereas it should be widely available. It has an extremely important place in Italian economic literature and the history of economic doctrines in general, and it is an essential source of knowledge of Pareto's economic and sociological theories. Several of Pareto's pupils preferred it to the *Manuale* since it was more accessible in character, form and content than the latter, especially for those used to current economics texts. It should certainly be studied before the *Manuale*.

In the *Manuale* Pareto's scope was wider and his consideration of problems more thorough, thus enabling him to establish the limits of economics more precisely. He benefited greatly from his use of mathematical analysis in his study of economics. The notions of particular economic equilibria in exchange, in production, etc., are analysed independently of each other and still show the influence of the models of those authors who inspired Pareto and the adaptation of mechanical paradigms to economics. These are superseded by the notion of a general economic equilibrium of the different kinds of transformation of economic goods: an equilibrium which results from a balance between what people want – their tastes – and the obstacles to the satisfaction of these tastes.

These elements are represented geometrically (topographically) with isometric preference curves and constraints similar to the level lines, isotherms and isobars, with surfaces which are similar to equipotential ones. They are analysed both separately and jointly, that is, at the intersection of their respective curves at the equilibrium point. They are studied in a way which allows theories of rational economics to give the most general view so far of the workings of the economy. Although we are thus able to get much closer to the reality of the economy than by means of theories which do not use these scientific tools of analysis, the theories of rational economics are still as far from reality as the theories of geometry, mechanics, physics, chemistry and biology are from their respective realities. The notion of capital, which was prominent in the *Cours* has been eliminated and the notion of price has also been partially eliminated; these have become auxiliary unknowns. The economic systems of exchange and production have been considered as being linked together by equations valid for points of equilibrium. Prices and coefficients of production are considered as variables as well as constants. The types of contract in monopoly and competition are linked to cases in which the economic actor to which the index function refers, either cannot or does not want to or can and does want to directly change the values of certain constants of the index function (prices, quantities). The maximum ophelimity, which has not been considered before, is dealt with together with the maximum profit for the monopolist. The notion of the maximum ophelimity for a community is developed. The allocation of production between several firms is analysed and the study of international trade taken up.

In the appendices to the *Manuale* and the *Manuel*, the mathematical analyses of various theories are elaborated together with their geometrical presentation. Pareto establishes the basis for a treatise on mathematical economics in the appendix to the *Manuel* in particular. He had been stimulated to expand his analysis by the great mathematician Volterra, whose authority served to quieten the doubts of many non-mathematicians. Volterra also provided the most refined and suitable instruments with which to develop economic analysis, indicating the shortcomings of the theories, demonstrating how to overcome them and suggesting how to develop the theories further. He gave examples of the most effective applications of mathematical analysis to the disciplines which had not been able to avail themselves of such tools or at least whose use of mathematics was limited.

Taking into account Fisher's observations on the impossibility of measuring pleasure directly, Pareto inverted Edgeworth's notion of indifference and preference lines (isophelime) so as to be able to eliminate, at least theoretically, the need to resort to the meta-economic notion of utility. This had been considered arbitrarily as a function which could be subjected to derivative and other types of analysis and was the basis for all the successive economics text books which dealt with the subject, including the *Cours*. Pareto theoretically eliminated from rational economics the need to treat non-measurable elements as quantities. He showed that it was possible to base the theories of economic equilibrium, whose foundations were then still not very solid, on a differential equation given by the observation of the fundamental act of choice on the part of economic actors. This was achieved with a series of indifference combinations admitting, at the most, the use of the meta-economic notion of ophelimity, just as that of force is admitted in mechanics in order to make the exposition of theories more comprehensible. Poincaré had suggested to Walras that the notion of an index of pleasure functions, of the type used by Cournot, might be useful. The systems of equations which determined economic equilibrium and their consequences are left unchanged, inasmuch as both in economics and mechanics the old road and the new lead to the same equilibrium equations. Pareto, going back to Cournot in a certain sense, caused rational analytical economics to take a step forward on the path traced by mathematics and physics and opened new horizons for economics. It was a step which can be compared to that made by infinitesimal calculus, when Cauchy's definition of infinitesimal as a variable size having zero as its limit took away the metaphysical considerations from this tool and thus paved the way for the development of modern science.

The *Cours* made more progress in a short time than those who had already witnessed the scientific advances made possible by Cournot's analysis and the new approach formulated by Walras had naturally expected. Pareto's *Manuel* was the source of a further advance in economic theory, demonstrating that we cannot unite under the heading of 'Lausanne school' three such different phases in the development of mathematical economics as Walras's *Eléments d'économic politique pure* and Pareto's *Cours* and *Manuel*. The *Manuel* is very different from the *Cours*, although since the *Manuel* refers to the *Cours*, the two works are complementary to each other and together form part of Pareto's progressive contribution to economic science, while their differences show how Pareto was continually developing this theories.

Not surprisingly, although Pareto the mathematical economist and the mathematicians who dealt with economics, understood each other, there was less mutual understanding between Pareto and the philosophers whose theories are for the most part non-experimental and extraneous to scientific movements. The most eminent Italian philosopher, Croce, recognised that mathematicians, who have a lively sense of the function of science, had made an important contribution to economic science by raising it to the dignity of abstract analysis. This had been obscured and suppressed by the mass of anecdotes emanating from the historical school. He maintained, however, that the mathematicians were wrong to believe that mathematics could approach the science of man, a form of conscious activity of man, in the same way as it rightly approached the empirical sciences of nature. Mathematical economists, however, think that in this field they are not mistaken and that their greatest merits are that they 'have a lively sense of the function of science' and of the 'dignity of abstract analysis'.

*   *   *

Pareto deals with mathematical statistics in the parts of the *Cours* (both the text and the additions) and the *Manuale* that discuss income curves and also in other works on the same subject both prior to and after the *Cours*, as well as in articles and communications and in the reference book on the application of interpolation formulas. He not only used statistical surveys as an inductive method or as documentation in his works, but also made original discoveries and contributed to refining the tools of statistical inquiry. These opened up new opportunities for statistical methodology which now occupies such an important place in the sciences in general.

Pareto's brilliant application of statistical method enabled him to establish the empirical law of the distribution of total income which goes by his name. The distribution curve has a very simple analytical expression. In the best-known part of its perimeter it varies very little in time and space and implies that an increase in minimum income and a decrease of inequality in the proportions of income cannot occur in isolation nor cumulatively without total incomes growing more rapidly than the population.

Unlike some literary figures who dramatically compared this law to the unveiling of the god of fortune, Pareto was merely satisfied that the law was able to explain many of his dearly held opinions and irrepressible feelings, in addition to the fact that through his discovery a statistical regularity was revealed. It was a legitimate satisfaction.

After the *Cours*, Pareto returned to the subject in the *Manuale*, demonstrating analytically that he was aware of the ingenious contributions to the theory of probability which could be made with his formula. This particularly applied to the consideration of incomes from wages, where he observed that studies often discovered average wages with divergencies that formed a curve which, though asymmetrical, was similar to the curve of statistical errors. He thought that using this analogy alone it was impossible to conclude that divergencies form along the curve of statistical errors and he observed that what was important was to have seen that a great variety of facts could be expressed approximately using a very simple formula. Later, and less importantly, it might be interesting to see how this formula could be deduced rationally from certain hypotheses on the distribution of qualities which enable people to obtain a certain income, but it must be emphasised that the form of the curve which the statistics provide us does not correspond at all to the probability curve, known as the curve of statistical errors, that is to the form the curve would have if the acquisition and conservation of wealth depended only on chance.

Pareto established, through his discovery, a solid basis for a new branch of investigative statistics and introduced an important chapter in the literature on methodology and applied statistics. The greatest economists and mathematical statisticians have measured themselves against it for the last forty years, so that dealing with this subject in international statistical literature has been seen as an honour and proof of capability.

Naturally, criticisms of Pareto's formula and the conclusions he drew from it soon appeared. Sometimes these were unfounded and due to errors of interpretation. Modifications, extensions, restrictions and exceptions were arrived at, which Pareto himself had solicited by making suggestions for research in which deviations from the general model could be found.

Despite Pareto's repeated repudiation, attempts were still made to deduce the general law of the distribution of income from considerations of probability and to demonstrate, within certain constraints, the law of the most probable distribution. These were abandoned when our greatest statistician raised the objection that these constraints could not have any real consistency, so the considerations of probability had to be restricted to the case of wages which Pareto himself had considered. Given the same constraints, assuming a relationship between income and the amount of work as given (which otherwise is more general), the general consensus realigned itself with Pareto and left others to change their minds as to whether Pareto's conclusions are tantamount to admitting that the distribution of income is a casual phenomenon, compatible with a constraint which depends on the form of the distribution of personal qualities and obstacles. As Pareto would observe, it is not a phenomenon to be imputed to chance in that the restrictions imposed on it deprive the statement of any value, because, he wrote, it can be concluded that the curve takes on a set form when the circumstances which cause it to take on another form are eliminated, or, rather, when certain constraints are imposed which lead to a desired form.

One of our best statisticians has concluded, however, that later studies have not undermined the principle: on the contrary they have further demonstrated the insight of its pioneering discoverer.

Pareto was interested in investigating the formulas of interpolation which have been widely applied in economics. They assuaged his love of mathematical analysis and enabled him to demonstrate that by using very simple methods, with the simplifying expedients that he suggested, the time series of economic data could be investigated and brought to life. In addition, these investigations suggested to Pareto the possibility of separating different kinds and lengths of movements in the time series of data and their graphic presentation with different degrees of interpolation. This is common nowadays, but sometimes it is misused in the research of so-called 'business cycles' undertaken by special offices which practise the art of separating secular movements, of liberating the series from the influence of seasonal fluctuations which sometimes exist only in the minds of researchers, or more exactly, in the formulas which they use to find them.

The research on interpolation gave rise to expectations, even on the part of Pareto, which so far have mainly remained unfulfilled. It was hoped that statistics, by the use of interpolation, would open up new fields of research into empirical laws and lead to progress in political economy. These empirical laws were to be compared with already established theoretical laws and pursue the discovery of new ones. The investigations into interpolation enabled Pareto, moreover, to make important considerations on statistical methodology as applied to the social sciences, considerations of his which should be kept in mind but are often forgotten. Pareto, above all, counselled prudence in coming to conclusions. He observed that the use of formulas of interpolation could be a help but could not be considered as a substitute for direct knowledge. It is well known that there are statisticians who undoubtedly prove their data with certain magic formulas of their own invention reminding one of those machines into which ingredients are put at one end and out of which pasta emerges at the other. Pareto was not a statistician of this kind and had no faith in such indices, nor did he waste time looking for them. He must have thought that if the application of formulas is not controlled and tested graphically, the interpretation of data is suspect: if methods to make data speak for themselves are not used, the data can be forced into strait-jackets and made to reveal what is already largely implicit in the formulas used, given their structure, as experience has shown.

Pareto proposed, as he wrote to us towards the end of his life, to take up his investigation into interpolation again and complete it. Maybe he had some ideas on the subject that nobody will ever know, although it seems likely he might have left notes that would have been interesting to look at had he not explicitly disposed otherwise.

* * *

It may be said that Pareto writes as a sociologist in all his major works: throughout the *Cours*, especially the second volume, 'The Economic Organism', chapter 1, 'General Principles of Social Evolution'; in volume III, 'Distribution and Consumption', chapter 1, 'The Income Curve', chapter 2, 'Social Physiology'; in *Systèmes socialistes*; and in the *Manuale*, chapter 1, 'General Principles', chapter 2, 'Introduction to Social Science', chapter 3, 'Population', chapter 9, 'The Concrete Economic Phenomenon'; in the *Mito virtuista*; and above all, naturally, in the three volumes of the

Trattato di sociologia generale, in the collected articles in the *Fatti e teorie* and other articles which were written before or after the *Trattato*.

In order to investigate the formation of Pareto's sociological theories and trace their development it would be useful to go back to pre-Paretian sociology, especially the areas that influenced Pareto most, and then proceed to study Pareto's sociological theories chronologically. We should proceed from the *Cours* to the *Systèmes*, to the *Manuale* and then to the *Trattato*, in order to see Pareto's development as a sociologist which culminated, if not in the above works, in the various theories and details which he put in order in the *Trattato*. However, to see Pareto's sociological theories displayed concisely we must proceed differently, we might almost say conversely.

The *Trattato*, which is the work in which the results of a lifetime's study of social life are to be found, is worth considering as fundamental. We shall also refer to those of his works which antedate it, in which any of the theories of the *Trattato* which we may wish to consider, are hinted at or elaborated.

Pareto differentiated the economic aspect from the rest of social life, but observing that there are no purely economic acts, he always kept the aspect he neglected in mind, as is witnessed by his considerations on the methodology of the social sciences, on the practical consequences of the regularities to be found in economic acts and certain sociological theories such as the mutual dependence of economic and social phenomena, the circulation of the élite, economic and social fluctuations, etc., which he had gradually developed before he dealt with sociology systematically.

Although some people raised their eyebrows and said, using university jargon, that Pareto had transferred to sociology, this was not the case. It was merely that he applied himself to it in a more systematic fashion. It might appear a transfer only to those who had not read, considered or remembered the content of Pareto's writings before the *Trattato*. Nor was there any foundation for the critical observation that the specific sociological theories that Pareto developed in the *Systèmes socialistes* and economic works such as the *Cours* and the *Manuale* before he managed to organise them all in the *Trattato*, were entirely out of place in the above economic writings. These sociological theories often served the purpose, in the author's plan, of fitting particular pieces of economic research into the wider field of social research.

Pareto had noticed that when what he called the logical experimental method was used to find regularities in social action, economic behaviour often appeared to be logical in that the means adopted seemed adequate in the situation. Even where this was not so, it was logical in part, sometimes the greater part. By virtue of this characteristic the study of economic behaviour is less difficult and enables economic theory to advance.

However, human actions in general are, for the most part, influenced by motives other than rationality. Pareto had already noted this in the *Systèmes* and in the *Manuale*. He reached the conclusion that sociology had to establish a theory of actions which are on the whole non-logical but are, however, capable of achieving a goal which may be logical. The distinction between logical and non-logical actions is not and never can be rigorous, and is therefore dubious, even untenable. However, Pareto has achieved his aim in making this distinction in that he attracted attention to and widened the study of a very large category of human action which occupies an important place in social life. This might not please the philosophers who, in fact, favour the extension of the field of logical action.

Pareto tried to found a sociology which distinguishes itself from the others. These forms of sociology had been created with aims that did not include the search for regularity in human actions or with methods that were applied erroneously. He therefore gathered a great deal of historical evidence to support his views and followed non-logical actions in the succession of doctrines in which usually non-logical actions are passed off as logical, according to one of the strongest human inclinations.

In the non-logical-experimental theories (c) Pareto discovers a not very variable part (a) and a very variable part (b). Part (a) is the principle which exists in the minds of men. Part (b) consists of the explanations given for this principle and the works it gives rise to. Part (a) corresponds to certain human impulses. Pareto's definition, however, does not include all of them. He observes that to determine social forms we must take interests into account. Pareto calls part (a) residues. He takes up the arguments he left off in the *Systèmes* and *Manuale*, on the objective and subjective aspects of theories, going back to the distinction made by Marx, which was, however, probably made earlier by the philosophical school which Marx himself drew on. It is well known that Pareto admired some of the Marx's penetrating sociological views. The distinction between subjective and objective reality can be useful for scientific research even if it gives rise to discussion among philosophers some of whom are certainly not very respectful of the refinements of high philosophy and have even denied the usefulness of this discussion. Pareto calls part (b) derivations. He calls part (c) derivatives, employing terms used in an analogous sense in philology.

Although Pareto was not the originator of the study of residues, he emphasised its importance and rendered it more specific. He distinguished six classes and numerous subdivisions of residues in order to facilitate their study: (1) instinct for combination, linked to innovation; (2) persistence of aggregates, which accounts for the stability of social circles; (3) the need to externalise feelings; (4) residues connected to sociality; (5) the integrity of the individual and his appurtenances; (6) sexual residues.

The logical-experimental sciences see derivations as manifestations of operative forces to be analysed in order to find out which operative forces the derivations correspond to. The non-logical-experimental sciences, on the other hand, think of derivations as being able to operate on the social makeup. Pareto divided them for practical purposes into four classes: (1) achievement; (2) authority; (3) agreement with sentiments and principles; (4) verbal proofs.

In the study of the properties of residues and derivations and their reciprocal actions, Pareto deals with the fluctuations of the residues which he had already discussed in the *Systèmes*. He notes the meagre influence of the derivations on the residues. He illustrates the importance of what Sorel had called myths. Sorel, with his mathematical training and interest in the economy, had understood Pareto the critic and philosopher of social movements, and the latter in turn appreciated Sorel. Pareto himself had talked to these myths in the *Systèmes* and the *Manuale*. He notes the social usefulness of certain doctrines which are devoid of experimental value (an idea already to be found in the *Manuale*) and, on the contrary, the minimum social usefulness of some experimentally based theories.

He takes up once more the theory of social heterogeneity and social circulation. This had already been touched on in the *Cours*, the *Systèmes* and the *Manuale* but was developed in the *Trattato* where the residues were taken into consideration.

Towards the end of the *Trattato*, which is a vast and well-documented work, perhaps the author felt like the artisan who speeds up towards the end of the job for fear of not finishing it. In this part Pareto deals with the general form of society, its elements and their mutual determination and the social states of dynamic (statistical) equilibrium which could perhaps be determined by systems of equations if it were possible to assign indices to all the elements and their actions. We are, however, far from being able to do this and no one can foresee how sociologists in the future might manage to do so. Maybe sociology, like biology until recently, lacks the necessary type of calculus.

In the meantime Pareto studied one of the properties of the social state: utility, of which he considered several kinds. He studied the maximisation of utility for the members or groups in a community and of the community as a whole differentiating between utility *of* and *for* a community. He argued that in sociology individuals could be considered collectively as compared to economics where only one individual is considered. He expanded on the use of force and shrewdness as arms of government; he dealt with stability and change in society, with economic and social periods, with the rhythm, the cyclical fluctuations in various social phenomena, expounding theories which originate in the *Cours*, the *Systèmes* and the *Manuale*. When considering social change, Pareto was anxious to point out that, like the historians Ferrari and Cattaneo, he started from the observation of reality. In this he was unlike Vico whose concepts he considered abstract and Spencer whose concepts he thought metaphysical. However, Pareto's considerations on trends in social phenomena helped to undermine the illusions which were spread by both scientific writings and popular belief about continual evolution, fatal progress, etc. These terms were ambiguous and divorced from reality (derivations) but tied to feelings which give them an almost religious force in periods of prosperity and caused them to fulfil an important social function. Pareto then moved from the investigation of the fluctuations of the derivations in relation to social fluctuations to the investigation of social equilibrium in history, applying the theory of residues to time, that is the variation in their distribution and particularly those of class 1 (instinct for combinations) and class 2 (persistence of aggregates) and their various proportions.

Throughout the *Trattato* and indeed throughout all his work, Pareto assembles and uses the facts gathered in the history of every epoch and every people in a masterly fashion, in order to prove and document his theories. He had studied this history and knew it better than some specialists who now quibble pedantically that what they call Pareto's historical forays are based on fragments. As though the history used in documenting sociological theories could be anything else but fragmentary! As though certain fragments in the correct light do not bring the past to life better than many colourless complete histories! As though, moreover, we did not know what tricks can be played with history that is not fragmentary but raised to a system of interpretation of the past. We have given here just a vague outline of Pareto's sociological theories which have been criticised for having a psychological basis, as if a study of human action could have any other basis.

In his *Trattato*, Pareto not only dealt with general sociological theories but illuminated other areas which he could not study in detail and which should form special chapters in sociology. He pointed out the gaps in these areas and hinted at the potential requirements of a study, such as one based on financial activities.

Several of Pareto's writings which ante-dated or post-dated the *Trattato* should be considered as applications of particular cases of sociological theories that Pareto was shaping in a general form. Ideas and theories already presented in the *Systèmes socialistes*, which saw the light of day

thirteen years before the *Trattato*, were re-examined, developed and
reorganised in the sociological system of the *Trattato*. Pareto studied the
theoretical systems and practical applications of socialism and selected the
common features among the wide variety of forms of certain human sentiments which explain the origins, success and failure of the different socialist systems and their different forms, in different places at different times,
but with particular emphasis on recent times. Pareto studied a particular
group of derivations in the *Systèmes socialistes* in depth, before he had
developed the theory of derivations and the residues which are linked to
them. It is a sharp, brilliant analysis in which the number of doctrines and
actions considered is overwhelming.

The *Mito virtuista* is basically an unbiased, cultivated, lively and sometimes ruthless study of the relationship between virtuosity and social utility.
Pareto does not consider this relationship to derive from intrinsic qualities
of virtuous acts. They are the result of whether or not certain sentiments
whose manifestations include virtuosity, exist. If they are superficial feelings of refusal their effect on society is useless. If they are so deep as to
instil sacrifice for a religion, an ideal, a country, a race, they can be useful
for society, and can characterise a strong, victorious, prosperous people. If
we observe the facts of history, Pareto says, we see that feelings of simple
refusal, of asceticism, have never distinguished a strong and powerful people. All peoples in whom ascetics predominated (unarmed prophets, as
Machiavelli would have called them) fell prey to conquerors. There has
never been a great, strong people in history that has manifested deep active
feelings who have not expressed themselves in an ideal, a faith, a religion
or a myth, as Sorel would have said. People have been seen to decay when
those feelings which they had expressed when they were great began to
weaken. Myths, however different their form, constitute the great forces
which form and develop human society since they respond to familiar,
valid sentiments despite their lack of logical content.

The same sociological theories are applied in the articles *Trasformazione
della democrazia* as in the *Trattato*. They look at the crisis of democracy,
with the breaking up of centralised power, the cycle of plutocracy and the
new feelings that prevail. The preface, which Pareto proposed to add to the
new edition of the *Trattato*, would have been on similar lines. In it he
wanted to investigate the sociological problems which were a result of the
war and, in particular, Fascism, whose beginnings Pareto himself witnessed. He observed Fascism and began to study it as an interesting experiment, seeing it as a proof of his sociological theories. He would have
eventually changed, developed or modified the latter, if necessary.

Pareto correctly cautioned about the limited value of forecasts in the area of social studies. In this field the regularities of observable circumstances are little known. Regularities always diverge more or less from reality, but in the case of social and economic action this divergence is great since they have to extend to future circumstances which are mostly unknown or unpredictable. Even if human action were to follow logical principles, it would nevertheless be difficult to make forecasts about it without the preventive knowledge of the circumstances in which decisions about the choice of human conduct took place. The impossibility of making forecasts in the field of human activity in general is understandable if an awareness of this defective or sparse knowledge is added to an awareness of the fact that human conduct is influenced by very varied and complex impulses of which we have only indirect evidence. Thus we can see the temptation of allowing the intuitions of men of action, which can be correct at times, to be substituted for the ill-founded conjectures of theoreticians.

However, Pareto in a well-known section of the *Trattato*, foreseeing the change in the economic and social movement which he was witness to, wrote that, by experimental deduction, it seemed to him more probable that an internal revolution would be followed by a new period of prosperity than that it would give power to individuals in whom class 2 residues were strong and who can and want to use force. But, he immediately added that these distant and uncertain events belong more to the realms of fantasy than to experimental science. By observing action and illuminating it by theory, Pareto was able to predict the course of human events with the help of an occasional surmise to which he did not give much weight.

It has been easier to criticise Pareto's sociology than it was to criticise his mathematical economics. Therefore numerous criticisms exist although they are not always as useful as those Pareto made of sociologists of the past. We have, of necessity, spent too little time on his sociological theories to be able to expand at this point on such criticisms.

No fundamental objection seems to have been raised about the difficulties of building experimental sociological theories on the basis of different elements of social life, impulses, actions and expressions when the only experimental datum is action (among which are expressions). Impulses which can be linked to actions are not, nor can they be, experimental data, however much the sensation exists of something which precedes action. It could thus be maintained that even impulses do not exist or at least are something which is greater than the reality of action.

It is, however, undeniable that Pareto's sociological system, which is the last of the great attempts to dominate the real web of human action theoretically, is the greatest and most penetrating of such bold attempts. Certainly Pareto, who started from partly experimental and partly metaphysical systems, has successfully tried to free theory from the latter and develop the former. Naturally the philosophers were very surprised and thought they had been insulted when they saw their sublime theories treated like the most common subject of study treated in the laboratory. They were reluctant to admit that a theory could be made from their theories and a science from their pretended absolute knowledge. They were rather piqued. They were probably worried too, lest the ground should be taken from under their feet due to an invasion of part of their field of action by the new science. This has taken the place of philosophy without the permission of the philosophers. Croce himself, who has been isolated from Italian spiritual life, in which he could have continued to play an important part, by an inexplicable and not very philosophic nostalgia for Giolitti, has joined the chorus of the critics of sociology. He has called it denigratingly 'the empirical science' and polemicising, with Pareto's sociology in particular, and has ostentatiously considered only the experimental aspect of sociological theory, purposely ignoring its logical aspects, that is, the highly philosophical content of the new science of society – or rather of the old science of man – which has taken a new name along with the new methods. This might have been unnecessary.

3 Pareto's General Equilibrium Equations

Alfonso de Pietri-Tonelli

It might be interesting to compare Pareto's general and definitive equations of economic equilibrium (Appendix of the *Manuel d'economie politique*, Paris, 1909) with (1) Cournot's equation of monopoly, trade and production (*Recherches sur les principes mathématiques de la théorie des richesses*, Paris, 1838); (2) Walras's equations of the equilibrium of exchange and production with a hypothesis of free competition (*Eléments d'économie politique pure*, 4th edition, Lausanne, 1900); (3) Pareto's own general equations of economic equilibrium, trade and production with free trade and monopoly (*Cours d'économie politique*, Volume I, Lausanne, (1896); (4) that in the text of his *Manuel*; and (5) the Appendix of the *Manuale*, in order to discover what the different systems being compared have in common and what is peculiar to each.

Let u be economic actors (traders, producers) and precisely: (1), (2), (3), ... (u): in general (k).

Let m be goods (products, services of capitals) and precisely: (A), (B), (C), ... (M), (N), ...

Of the m goods: n are used in production and precisely: (A), (B), (C), ... and in general (I); or o are produced and precisely: (M), (N), ... and in general (J).

(A) is used as numeraire in any case.

Let the quantities traded of (A), (B), ... (M), ... by single traders (1), (2), be respectively: a_1, a_2, ... b_1, ... m_1, ... n_1......; let them altogether be: A, B, ... M, N, ... Let the total quantity of (A) traded with (B) be: A_b, of (A) against (C) be: A_c, ... of (B) against (A): B_a, ...

For single traders let the initial quantities of (A), (B), ... be respectively: a_1^0, a_2^0, ... b_1^0, ...; let the quantities consumed of (A), (B), ... (M), ... be respectively: a_1', a_2', ... b_1', ... m_1', ... and the same quantities at an equilibrium point be represented by: $\mathbf{a}_1'$, $\mathbf{a}_2'$, ... $\mathbf{b}_1'$, ... $\mathbf{m}_1'$, ...

Let the prices be indicated of (A), (B), ... (M), ... expressed by (A), by: $p_a(a)$ $(=1)$ $p_b(a)$ .... $p_m(a)$ or more simply, having taken (A) as numeraire, by

$p_a, p_b, ... p_m, ...$ and the prices of (A), (B) ...., (M), ... in (B) are represented in a similar fashion by: $p_a(b), p_b(b) (=1), p_c(b), ... p_m(b), ...$ and so on.

The elementary ophelimities are characterised in general, for (1) as regards (A), (B), ... (M) ..., for (2) as regards (A) ..., respectively by:

$$\frac{\partial I_1}{\partial a_1}, \frac{\partial I_1}{\partial b_1}, ... \frac{\partial I_1}{\partial m_1}, ... \frac{\partial I_2}{\partial a_2}, ...$$

The weighted elementary ophelimities will be found analogously by:

$$\frac{1}{p_b}\frac{\partial I_1}{\partial b_1}, ... \frac{1}{p_m}\frac{\partial I_1}{\partial m_1}, ... \frac{1}{p_b}\frac{\partial I_2}{\partial b_2}, ...$$

Let the quantities of (A), (B).... provided to the firms producing be denoted by: A'', B'',..... and for an equilibrium position $\mathbf{A}''$, $\mathbf{B}''$, ... The quantities effectively transformed by productive industries are A''', B''', ... and $\mathbf{A}'''$, $\mathbf{B}'''$, ... Let the quantities consumed of (M) (N), ... be respectively: M'', N'', ... and $\mathbf{M}'''$, $\mathbf{N}'''$, ...

The coefficients of production (M), (N), ... be represented by: m_a, m_b, ... n_a, n_b, ...

The unit costs of (M), (N), ... be depicted by q_m, q_n ...... and the total costs by Q_m, Q_n, ...

The advantage of trader (2) having monopoly (B) be indicated by a_2. The advantage of producer (2) with monopoly (N), be represented by A_2.

The equations of Cournot. Equation of the monopoly of trade of (B)

$$B + p_b\frac{\partial B}{\partial p_b} = 0.$$

Equation of the monopoly of production (N)

$$N + \frac{dN}{dp_n}\left(p_n - \frac{dQ_n}{dN}\right) = 0$$

The equations of Walras. Equilibrium of trade with free competition

(1)
$$\begin{cases} \displaystyle\sum_{i-b,c,d,\;\text{K}} A_i = \sum_{\substack{I=B,C,D,\;\text{K} \\ i=b,c,d,\;\text{K}}} I_a p_i(a) \\[2em] \displaystyle\sum_{i=a,c,d,\;\text{K}} B_i = \sum_{\substack{I=A,C,D,\;\text{K} \\ i=a,c,d,\;\text{K}}} I_b p_i(b) \end{cases}$$

. . . .

(2)
$$\begin{cases} I_a = F_{ia}(p_b(a), p_c(a), p_d(a),\;\text{K}) \quad \left(\begin{smallmatrix} I=B,C,\;\text{K} \\ i=b,c,\;\text{K} \end{smallmatrix}\right) \\[1em] I_b = F_{ib}(p_a(b), p_c(b), p_d(b),\;\text{K}) \quad \left(\begin{smallmatrix} I=A,C,\;\text{K} \\ i=a,c,\;\text{K} \end{smallmatrix}\right) \end{cases}$$

. . . .

(3)
$$\begin{cases} p_a(b) = \dfrac{1}{p_b(a)}, p_c(b) = \dfrac{p_c(a)}{p_b(a)}, p_d(b) = \dfrac{p_d(a)}{p_b(a)},\text{K} \\[1.5em] p_a(c) = \dfrac{1}{p_c(a)}, p_b(c) = \dfrac{p_b(a)}{p_c(a)}, p_d(c) = \dfrac{p_d(a)}{p_c(a)},\text{K} \end{cases}$$

	Equations:	Numbers of	Unknowns:
(1)	$m-1$	$p_a(b), p_a(c), \ldots p_b(a) \ldots$	$m(m-1)$
(2)	$m(m-1)$	$A_b, A_c, \ldots B_a, B_c \ldots$	$m(m-1)$
(3)	$(m-1)(m-1)$		
	$2m(m-1)$		$2m(m-1)$

Equilibrium of production with free competition

[1] $I = F_i(p_a, p_b, \text{K } p_m, p_n \text{ K})$ $\left(\begin{smallmatrix} I=A,B,\text{K} \\ i=a,b,\text{K} \end{smallmatrix}\right)$

[2] $J = F_i(p_a, p_b, \text{K } p_m, p_n \text{ K})$ $\left(\begin{smallmatrix} J=M,N,\text{K} \\ j=m,n,\text{K} \end{smallmatrix}\right)$

[3] $p_j = \displaystyle\sum_{i=a,b,c,\text{K}} p_i j_i$ $(j = m,n,\text{K})$

[4] $I = \displaystyle\sum_{\substack{j=m,n,\text{K} \\ J=M,N,\text{K}}} j_i J$ $\left(\begin{smallmatrix} I=A,B,\text{K} \\ i=a,b,\text{K} \end{smallmatrix}\right)$

Numbers of

Equations:			Unknowns:
[1]	n	$A, B, \ldots\ldots\ldots\ldots$	n
[2]	$o-1$	$M, N, \ldots\ldots\ldots\ldots$	o
[3]	o	$p_b, p_c, \cdots p_m, \cdots$	
[4]	n		$n+o-1$

$$2n + 2o - 1 \qquad\qquad\qquad\qquad 2n + 2o - 1$$

Equations in *Cours*. Equilibrium of trader with free competition and constant prices:

(I) $\quad \dfrac{\partial I_k}{\partial a_k} = \dfrac{1}{p_b}\,\dfrac{\partial I_k}{\partial b_k} = \ldots \qquad\qquad (k = 1, 2, 3, \ldots u)$

(II) $\quad \displaystyle\sum_{i=a,b,c,\ldots} p_i i_k = 0 \qquad\qquad\qquad (k = 1, 2, 3, \ldots u)$

(III) $\quad \displaystyle\sum_{k=1}^{k=u} i_k = 0 \qquad\qquad\qquad\qquad (i = a, b, c, \ldots)$

Numbers of

Equations:			Unknowns:
(I)	$(m-1)\,u$	$a_1, a_2, \ldots b_1, b_2, \ldots$	mu
(II)	u	$p_b, p_c, \ldots\ldots\ldots\ldots$	$m-1$
(III)	$m-1$		

$$mu + m - 1 \qquad\qquad\qquad\qquad mu + m - 1$$

Monopoly of (2) in trade of (*B*)

$$p_b + b_2 \frac{\partial p_b}{\partial b_2} = 0$$

equation to put in place of one of the (I).

Equilibrium of production with free competition and constant prices.

(I) $\dfrac{\partial I_k}{\partial a_k} = \dfrac{1}{p_b}\dfrac{\partial I_k}{\partial b_k} = \dots \dfrac{1}{p_m}\dfrac{\partial I_k}{\partial m_k} = \dots$ $(k = 1,2,\dots u)$

(II) $\displaystyle\sum_{i=a,b,\dots} p_i i_k - \sum_{j=m,n,\dots} p_j j_k = 0$ $(k = 1,2,\dots u)$

(III) $p_j = \displaystyle\sum_{i=a,b,\dots} p_i j_i$ $(j = m,n,\dots)$

(IV) $I = \displaystyle\sum_{\substack{j=m,n,\dots \\ J=M,N,\dots}} j_i J$ $\begin{pmatrix} I = A,B,\dots \\ i = a,b,\dots \end{pmatrix}$

Numbers of

	Equations:		Unknowns:
(I)	$(n + o - 1)\,u$	$a_1, a_2, \dots b_1, b_2, \dots m_1, \dots$	$(n + o)\,u$
(II)	u	$p_b, p_c, \dots p_m \dots$	$n + o - 1$
(III)	o		
(IV)	$n - 1^*$		

$(n + o)\,u + n + o - 1$ $(n + o)\,u + n + o - 1$

Monopoly of (2) in the production of (*N*).

$$p_n - q_n + N\dfrac{dp_n}{dN} = 0,$$

equation to be put in place of one of the [IV].

The equations of the Appendix of the *Manuel*. *Note*: We do not deal with the general equilibrium equations of the Appendix of the *Manuale*, which, although using symbols similar to those of the equations of the Appendix of the *Manuel*, correspond to those of the text of the *Manuale* and the *Manuel* in the way the equilibrium is determined and are reminiscent therefore of the *Cours*.

---

*As one equation has been eliminated from (1), [2], (III) of the previous systems, respectively, one of [IV] follows from others because $I = \Sigma i_k$ and $J = \Sigma j_k$, so that the number of independent equations contained in [IV] is only $n - 1$.

Equilibrium of trade with free competition and constant prices.

(a) $\quad \dfrac{\partial l_k}{\partial a'_k} = \dfrac{1}{p_b} \dfrac{\partial l_k}{\partial b'_k} = \ldots$ $\qquad (k = 1,2,\ldots u)$

(b) $\quad \displaystyle\sum_{i=a,b,\ldots} p_t(i'_k - i^0_k) = 0$ $\qquad (k = 1,2,\ldots,u-1)$

(c) $\quad \displaystyle\sum_{k=1}^{k=u} (i'_k - i^0_k) = 0$ $\qquad (i = a,b,\ldots)$

	Equations:	Numbers of	Unknowns:
(a)	$u(m-1)$	$a'_1, a'_2, \ldots b'_1, \ldots$	mu
(b)	$u-1$	$p_b, p_c \ldots\ldots\ldots\ldots\ldots$	$m-1$
(c)	m		
	$mu + m - 1$		$mu + m - 1$

Monopoly of (2) in trade of (B).
Maximum ophelimity for the monopolist (2):

$$\frac{dI_2}{dp_b} = 0.$$

Maximum revenues in money for the monopolist (2):

$$\frac{da_2}{dp_b} = 0.$$

Either one or the other of the preceding equations is to be put in place of (a) which is missing.

Equilibrium of trade and production with free competition and constant (and variable) prices and constant coefficients of production.

(A) $\quad \dfrac{\partial I_k}{\partial \mathbf{a}'_k} = \dfrac{1}{p_b}\dfrac{\partial I_k}{\partial \mathbf{b}'_k} = \ldots = \dfrac{1}{p_m}\dfrac{\partial I_k}{\partial \mathbf{m}'_k} = \ldots$ $\qquad (k = 1, 2, \ldots u)$

(B) $\quad \displaystyle\sum_{i=a,b,\ldots} p_i(\mathbf{i}'_k - i^0_k) + \sum_{j=m,n,\ldots} p_j \mathbf{j}'_k = 0$ $\qquad (k = 1, 2, \ldots, u)$

(C) $\quad \begin{cases} \displaystyle\sum_{k=1}^{k=u}\left(i^0_k - \mathbf{i}'_k\right) = \mathbf{I}'' \\[2em] \displaystyle\sum_{k=1}^{k=u}\mathbf{j}'_k = \mathbf{J}'' \end{cases}$ $\qquad \begin{array}{l}\left(\begin{array}{l} i = a, b, \ldots \\ I = A, B, \ldots\end{array}\right) \\[2em] \left(\begin{array}{l} j = m, n, \ldots \\ J = M, N, \ldots\end{array}\right)\end{array}$

Constant Prices:

(D) $\quad p_j J'' = \mathbf{Q}_j$ $\qquad \left(\begin{array}{l} j = m, n, \ldots \\ J = M, N, \ldots\end{array}\right)$

Variable Prices:

(D′) $\quad \displaystyle\int_0^{J''} p_j\, d\mathbf{J}'' = \mathbf{Q}_j$ $\qquad \left(\begin{array}{l} j = m, n, \ldots \\ J = M, N, \ldots\end{array}\right)$

(E) $\quad \mathbf{I}'' = \mathbf{I}'''$ $\qquad (I = A, B, \ldots)$

	Equations:	Number of	Unknowns:
(A)	$(n + o - 1)\,u$	$a'_1, a'_2, \ldots b'_1, \ldots m'_1, \ldots$	$(n + o)\,u$
(B)	u	$p_b, p_c, \ldots p_m \cdots$	$n + o - 1$
(C)	$n + o$	$A'', B'' \ldots\ldots\ldots\ldots\ldots$	n
(D) or (D′)	o	$M'', N'' \ldots\ldots\ldots\ldots\ldots$	o
(E)	$n - 1*$		
	$(n + o)(u + 2) - 1$		$(n + o)(u + 2) - 1$

N.B. In *Lezioni di scienze economica razionale e sperimentale* (Rovigo, 1st edition, 1919; 2nd edition, with preface by Vilfredo Pareto, 1921) during lectures and here also, we have re-established the equality of the number of unknowns and the number of equations, removing from the latter an iden-

---

*One of (E) is not independent, so that the number of independent equations contained in (E) is $o - 1$.

28   *Vilfredo Pareto*

tity. This had either been placed among the equations of the *Manuel* (Appendix), erroneously or had insinuated itself there due to an oversight which nobody had noticed. Clearly the author of the *Manuel* agreed immediately to remove it.

Monopoly of (2) in the production of (*N*):

Maximum ophelimity for the monopolist (2): $\dfrac{dI_2}{dp_n} = 0.$

Maximum revenues in money for the monopolist (2)

$$\frac{dA_2}{dp_n} = 0.$$

Either one or the other of the preceding equations is used to give the extra unknown A_2.

Final Considerations: The features which the systems under comparison have in common and their differences are too evident to be indicated one by one: the rapid evolution of the general mathematical theory of economic equilibrium from Walras to Pareto is obvious if only on account of the similarity of its symbols which we have established where possible. This was the intention of this brief note.

Finally, it may be seen that similar and more extensive comparisons can be established for the other particular equilibrium equations in the Appendix of the *Manuel*: in any case, the original contributions of the different authors and their different works to the history of theory remain obvious.

4 Pareto and Socialism

Georges H. Bousquet

The spread of a doctrine owes little to its logical value. Moreover, those who think that they can judge from the logical value of a particular doctrine what its social effects will be, lay themselves open to great errors.

Pareto, (*Systèmes socialistes* I, 16)

So far, we have studied Pareto's approach to economic problems. In this chapter, we will examine his sociological theories. In doing so, we consider his critique of socialism, 'critique' being understood in its etymological sense. This approach is all the more justified in that Pareto coupled his study of sociology with a study of socialism; his *Systèmes socialistes* was in fact the precursor of the *Trattato di sociologia generale*. In the *Systèmes* one can see the early forms of many concepts which he developed later on. The work by Pareto that deals most fully with socialism is the *Systèmes*. Then come a handful of articles and his 'Introduction to K. Marx's *Capital*' (extracts published by Guillaumin).[1] We will consider the most recent types of socialism in Chapter 6, and restrict ourselves here to more general questions.

Les Systèmes socialistes is a brilliant and profound book, but unfortunately it lacks any consistent structure. This fault was pointed out when the work was first published, particularly in reviews by de Foville (*Economie journal*) and Gide (*Revue d'économie politique*): 'It is difficult', wrote Gide, 'to find any unifying factor in the various chapters.' We will try to restore a logical structure to the book, without concealing the fact that the author himself scatters the diverse strands of his thought throughout.

Pareto explains the goal which he set himself thus: 'On the one hand, we will attempt to identify the tangible factors which have favoured the rise of certain social systems, or the conception of envisaged social systems; in other words, the factors that a study of these systems reveals. On the other hand, we will examine the arguments which have been used to justify these actual or projected systems, and we will see to what extent the premises are drawn from experience and logical deduction.' (*Ss* I, 16) Thus, (in *Les Systèmes socialistes*) he is dealing with two quite different areas: firstly, sociological research; secondly, studies on the logico-experimental value of certain lines of argument. Pareto, as he went on to do in the *Trattato*, combines the two approaches. In fact it is rare, in formulating a given system, that he tackles both sides of the question, although there are exceptions (such as the 'cult of nature' in the eighteenth century; *Ss* II, 21ff.). Furthermore, in the *Systèmes* Pareto often considers areas which do not relate directly to his planned framework. All this does not make for an easy *scientific* understanding of the work, so there is a danger of such comprehension being lost in an appreciation of the ironic style – the irony is superb but entirely external – behind which thought of great depth is concealed.

We will start by considering the second of the two problems mentioned above.

I

If you tell me that a man can live for 200 years just by eating a thyme leaf every day, I will not be forced into the dilemma of either accepting your statement or finding another means of prolonging life for 200 years.

Pareto (*Ss* II, 103)

What, then, is the logical and experimental value of socialist theories and doctrines? We will not spend time over a detailed definition of what constitutes a socialist system. Such questions of definitions are not very interesting (I, 110ff.). In general terms, one can state that these theories are concerned with limiting or suppressing private property (see *Is.*) but, adds Pareto, private property is limited under all regimes, particularly by taxation: 'This fact can scarcely be denied, but people refuse to acknowledge the consequences of this, saying that the levies imposed on private property by existing regimes are different from socialist levies, because the first ones are simply taxes. This is a classification not on the basis of things, but on the basis of names with which one embellishes these things.'

The study of socialist doctrines demonstrates that they are most often without any logical or scientific value. Pareto shows the errors and sophisms that they conceal, though he also points out the grain of truth they contain. His criticisms can be put into three main categories (although, of course, he did not make this distinction anywhere; we are attempting to construct a logical framework for his thought, as we did in our *précis* for sociology). These three categories are: (a) verbal derivations; (b) economic errors; (c) sociological errors.

Derivations[2]

Pareto analyses with great care many concepts on which socialist theories are based. He shows that it is impossible to reason logically when using such concepts. 'For example, men in general want freedom and fear constraint. The first word has agreeable associations, unlike the second, which has unpleasant ones. The way to make people accept coercion, would be to call it freedom' (I, 324). This can be achieved by means of much sophistry. But this type of argument, as Pareto demonstrates, relies on sentiment, not logic. For example, a distinction is made between 'true' and 'false' freedom; this vague word lends itself to any number of attractive arguments, etc.

The same is true of the epithet 'natural', which lends itself to many derivations. Ch. Andler wrote: 'For poverty to be natural, would it not also have to be general?' Pareto commented: 'How could such a fine mind possibly have stumbled across such gross sophistry? There is only one possible explanation: his faith has blinded him.' This argument has as its premise: 'All that is not general is not natural.' But that is absurd. One could also say like Andler: 'For women's beauty to be natural, would it not also have to be general? If there were ugly women, then beauty would not be natural' (II, 85). Moreover, the word 'natural' is not defined. These arguments depend on words and the feelings they evoke, not on external reality.

Another good derivation – this time juridical – is that of natural rights, which several authors, such as Fourier, accord to men.[3] Pareto examines the value of these 'natural rights' of which people in our society are deprived and comes to the conclusion that the four natural rights of Fourier are worth 1.83 francs per annum to each proletarian! (II, 255).

Pareto rigorously analyses the term 'solidarity', so much in vogue at the beginning of the twentieth century. This word has at least three meanings. He points to the failure to make a distinction between the undoubted fact that human beings are mutually dependent and the assertion that this mutual dependence should be encouraged as something good and beneficial. Gide quotes a passage from Carlyle in which a poor Irish widow demonstrated society's common membership of the human race by passing on fatal typhoid fever to the community that had rejected her – she and those who had rejected her were equally human. Pareto replies (II, 231): 'Any proof that the widow was "the flesh of their flesh" is totally non-existent. A rat carrying the plague could use exactly the same language.' He shows this by adapting the passage by Carlyle to the case of the rat. He devotes many pages to the subject of solidarity.

It would be a mistake, however, to think that the *Systèmes* is an attack on
the value of socialist ideas. Pareto directs his trenchant critique against liberal optimism as well, for it uses the same sophistry. 'All these axioms
which use vague terminology do not mean anything at all, and therefore
can mean anything one likes. No one knows exactly what are the 'great
providential laws' of Bastiat, so according to what one thinks they are, his
axiom can be taken to mean entirely different things' (II, 50). His theory on
service-value is based on the same equivocations (II, 52ff.).

This appears even more clearly in the tedious, endless quarrelling by
Proudhon and Bastiat over the 'legitimacy of interest': 'Neither of these
two adversaries feels the need to give a rigorous definition of the terms
"interest on capital" and "legitimate" when arguing whether there is or is
not an appropriate relationship between the two terms' (I, 359). In short,
these analyses, of which we are only giving a few examples, show the
futile logic behind the numerous arguments used in support of economic
and social doctrines. But these doctrines contain additional errors.

Economic errors

The socialist doctrines are not only very vague; their proponents have also
made some very serious economic errors. Pareto makes this particularly
clear with regard to the problem of interest, but in line with his usual
'method', his exposition appears in five or six different places in the book.
Initially (I, 360f.), he gives a remarkable classical analysis of the role of
capital in a normal society and in a socialist society. He shows which part
of production in a society could in fact be appropriated by capitalists and
under what conditions, identifying two distinct meanings of the word 'capital'. He then shows that the idea of 'capital' according to Proudhon is
related to a third concept (I, 388ff.). But it is in another chapter that he discusses his (Proudhon's) idea for free credit (II, 275ff.) making its absurdity
all too clear: 'The problem with treating future wealth as if it were current
wealth', he states, 'is that it then becomes useless to save for production. If
only one could sow the field with the wheat of the next harvest, that would
indeed be a real achievement'. The conclusion drawn from these premises
is false, therefore the premises themselves are wrong, as he has
demonstrated.

Pareto devotes the last two chapters of the *Systèmes* to Marx, and they
are without doubt the most interesting in the book. He counters the economic theories of that writer with his own more precise sociological theories. Marx's errors and omissions are mercilessly underscored. In the

'Introduction to *Capital*' the idea that value is 'crystallised work' (that value derives solely from labour) is brilliantly criticised. In the *Systèmes*, the illogicality of the theory of 'surplus value' is virulently attacked. After a rigorous discussion, Pareto launches this stinging satire: (II, 388) 'Surplus value can have no other origin than the worker. This is bizarre... In India, elephants are used to unload beams from a cart. The entrepreneur in charge of this operation cannot appropriate any surplus value since the elephants do not produce any. But if he used workers, then surplus value would appear. Do we then have to extend to all living creatures the production of surplus value? Life would be curious if so.... A cook can have his roasting-spit turned by a paid child, by a big dog, or by machinery. If he has it done by the child, he can appropriate surplus value. But this will be doubtful if he uses a dog and impossible if he has a mechanical roasting-spit. It has to be admitted that the influence of the motor driving the spit is hard to understand.'[4]

Other economic theories are also criticised, such as the 'fund for wages', etc. (II, 300ff.). Pareto also devotes an interesting paragraph to the problem of distribution (II, 160ff.). Firstly, he argues that in principle inheritance is a very imperfect way of distributing wealth. 'Therefore the way is clear for well-intentioned reformers. However, they should not limit themselves to the easy role of criticising the existing system' but should show that their proposals are preferable to the present system. They should do several things: (1) they should express themselves clearly and precisely. This did not happen very often; (2) There was a psychological problem in that the new method of distribution ought to be compatible with human nature; (3) It should be established that the necessary type of government was a possibility. This was a political problem; (4) Another psychological problem was stated thus: 'It should be shown that the new system of distribution will ensure human happiness and it should not be forgotten that such happiness is essentially subjective. Therefore, it is a matter of ensuring happiness such as it is understood by people in general and not as it would be defined by some would-be reformer'; (5) This question was linked to some very complex economic problems concerning the relation between production and distribution which we will not go into here; (6) Lastly, either one recognised the existence of certain principles of justice and equity that transcended the organisation of society, in which case the reformers had to demonstrate that their policies were in accordance with these principles, or one believed – as in Marxism for example – that these principles existed in direct relation to the organisation of society, in which case another problem arose: the new method of distribution would modify the principles accepted by men. This would have repercussions on their idea of happiness, and doubtless on production too. Would these effects be outweighed by the advantages of the new method of distribution? A rapid glance at a few of the proposals for distribution would show that the reformers did not take these questions into account and that their ideas lacked any clarity.

Sociological errors

Not only should the reformers base their arguments on reality rather than on words; not only should they examine economic facts with greater care, but they should have sociological problems to resolve. Again, more often than not, he says, their ideas are either inadequate or non-existent. Pareto contrasts (II, 1f.) Aristotle's common sense with Plato's chimeras. In several other places, he points out the general problems that the socialists should of necessity resolve.

One example is the problem of selection (II, 134): 'All human societies contain elements which are incapable of fitting into the normal conditions of life, and if the activities of these elements are not kept within certain limits, society will be destroyed.' Socialists ought to be concerned with this question, which is difficult to resolve. Indeed, humanitarian sentiments are opposed to the necessity of selection, and yet, up to a certain point, they are useful to society. This, then, is the problem to be resolved: (1) Can the number of births of social misfits be lowered? (2) If not, how can they be eliminated with a minimum of wrong choices, a minimum of suffering and without damaging the humanitarian sentiments whose development is useful to society? (II, 150). This is a scientific problem, but the reformers are neglecting certain of its aspects.

Another question concerns the choice of the right persons. Here the arguments of the reformers (I, 273ff.) are analogous to those they use with regard to distribution. The present system for selection on the basis of abilities is seriously defective, but it has yet to be shown that the proposed system is better. If one analyses the ideas of Plato, Comte, and Saint-Simon, one could argue that they avoided the real problem, and that, from a positivist viewpoint, their precepts had no value.

Furthermore, the reformers want to unify everything. Is this good or bad? One must make a distinction. (I, 292ff.). There is some truth in their ideas. 'In certain cases, unity is just about essential; in others, it is very useful. This gives support to the proponents of comprehensive uniformity', but just because something is true in certain cases, one cannot say that it must therefore be true in all instances. An examination of the facts also proves this. The problem is one of quantity rather than of quality. Pareto's discussion of this is worth quoting, in particular when it comes to epigrammatic comment: 'Each new reformer does not fully realise that, if his predecessors had achieved a unified organisation of society, he would not have been able to formulate his system. Brunetière shares with Comte a love of unity and a hatred of 'disorderly individualism'.

If Comte were still alive, though, and locked up with Brunetière, one could fear that they would end up by destroying each other, whilst, thanks to freedom, they could write as much as they wanted, and the loss to society would be just a few reams of paper and some printing expenses.

One also finds (says Pareto, I, 347, etc.) reading Saint-Simon, and even Marx and Engels, supposed historical laws which, from the point of view of social evolution, bear no relation to actual truth.

To sum up, our reformers produce sociological errors in abundance. Should it be said, then, that they are of no value whatsoever? That would be to overstate the case since quite often their work contains fragments of truth – even Fourier's for example (II, 274). It is above all in the works of Marx that we find highly valuable sociological analysis. For instance, it is thanks to historical materialism (II, 400ff.) that we have an analysis of historical and social phenomena which had been neglected until Marx and Engels, 'Class struggle', as Pareto took great pains to show, is a quasi-scientific concept. Marx was only in error in over-emphasising class conflict.

Except for these few points, socialist doctrines are not of great value, or even of no value at all, as theories. Is this to say that, to Pareto, socialism was only a series of 'systems' which are more or less preposterous?

Carried away by hatred and injustice, Arturo Labriola defended this ridiculous idea.[5] In contrast to the methods of Labriola, for whom assertions took the place of proof, let the Master himself speak. After the passage which we quoted earlier (p. 29), he expresses himself thus (I, 16): 'Unfortunately the extent to which certain topics are covered in this book cannot correspond to their practical importance. This gives rise to the thought that an objective study only might have had its advantages.... The study of the logical value of these arguments, which forms a large part of this book, is curious and interesting as a piece of philosophical speculation, but has only a very slight practical importance.' He returns several times to this idea: 'The fact that we have spent a long time examining the value of, looked at logically, certain ideas, does not mean that their consideration is of great practical value'. (I, 268)[6] Consequently, there is something more in socialism than these 'systems born of rationalising reason', as Labriola put it. Pareto does not only state this, he proves it, as we shall go on to see.

II

In considering socialism, we must first of all distinguish between theories and facts. As regards the facts, we must look afresh at the distinction between the actual measures to restrict private property and the realities that the theories concerning this conceal. Pareto was concerned above all with the second problem, but he also studied 'real systems'. His study of 'state socialism' in Greece and Rome showed the economic consequences of the destruction of personal property (I, 150ff.). As for the partial creation of small communist societies, this had been possible only because of the strong affinities that linked their members together.

Pareto continuously emphasises the great importance of sentiment in societies and the minimal importance of logic. If one pays attention to people's sentiments rather than to their arguments, he says, one understands the intrinsically invariable foundation that is unchanged by the different forms of interpretations imposed upon it (rationalisations, derivations). It is therefore important to identify the sentiments expressed by socialist doctrines and the realities they reveal.

The success of socialist ideas in different social classes comes from the concurrence between the sentiments of that class and the tendencies of the doctrine. Pity is a very common sentiment 'which leads men to identify with the suffering of their fellow men, and to try to alleviate it. This sentiment is most respectable and most useful to society, and in truth, is its cement' (I, 62). This sentiment is the basis for almost all socialist doctrines. But it is not the sole reason for their success and development. In the lower classes of society, we find yet other tendencies which explain the spread of such ideas, tendencies which are very different from those observable in the upper classes. Among the lower classes, there is a sentiment which 'originates in the suffering endured by the members of these classes, and in the desire they feel to put an end to it by seizing the riches enjoyed by people in the upper classes; or it originates simply because they covet what other people have' (I, 65). Socialist doctrines articulate this sentiment for the lower classes and are accepted by such people for this reason, and not for their logico-experimental value. As for the success of socialism amongst the upper classes, this is explicable largely by a deterioration in the sentiment of pity, corresponding to a general degeneration in these classes. Taking everything into consideration, it is necessary to distinguish between the psychology of the lower classes and that of the upper classes. It is useful that the latter have a benevolent attitude towards the former, but any excess in this tendency would be harmful and a sign of degeneration. Throughout the ages, humanitarian sentiments have given birth to sentimental dreams. It is important to examine the resonance of these ideas. If they are only welcomed by a small number of poets and writers, it shows that the élite is full of vigour and energy. But as an élite declines into decadence, this 'reasoning' gains more and more success. This social phenomenon had been observed throughout the centuries in Rome and in pre-revolutionary France.

Therefore the psychological realities on which socialism is founded are highly variable, according to the different social classes. Pareto could also have emphasised the fact that they vary in different countries at a single moment in time (*Is*, 2); this proves *a fortiori* that their logical content can tell us scarcely anything about the concrete aspects of social phenomena.

Socialism covers still more things, appetites and interests. Interests and sentiments are indeed the major forces which influence societies: 'Another origin of socialism amongst élites is to be found in the interest of one part of an élite. No social class is homogeneous. Each one contains certain rivalries, and any of the factions which is formed in this way can try to find support among the lower classes. This is a very common phenomenon... In addition, it often happens that, when a doctrine has many followers, when certain sentiments are very common, people think that it is clever to make use of this doctrine or these sentiments by keeping to the outward form while changing the substance' (I, 72). Pareto demonstrated that this fact was not unique to socialist doctrine, but that one could observe it under other conditions.

Thus one should not confuse form and substance. Even less should one confuse variations in form with variations in substance. Doctrines can change, whereas sentiments change little. Thus in the Middle Ages and even later, doctrines or 'derivations' tended to take the form of religion. Today, explanatory reasoning more easily fits into a scientific framework: 'Scientific socialism is born out of a need to give a scientific face to humanitarian aspirations. In our age, the scientific form has become fashionable, in much the same way as the religious form was in the past' (I, 74).

Let us now examine variations in social phenomena, in particular regarding sentiments; one can observe that major social trends do not unfold uniformly, but rather through a series of waves of more or less rhythmic oscillatory movements. For example, in the course of time the periods of belief and unbelief alternate successively. This makes the prediction of social trends very difficult and uncertain. At this point, the economist may be of some help to the historian of ideas, or better, to the sociologist. Indeed, the income curve drew Pareto's attention to the distribution of psychological characteristics amongst men. He observed that this distribution was irregular, and that consequently it tended to place every individual at a definite level in the 'social pyramid', to use imprecise but convenient imagery. This tendency was, moreover, echoed by others. 'If men are arranged according to their different levels of power and social influence, they will be, at least in part, the same men who will occupy the same place in this distribution structure and in that of the distribution of wealth' (I. 28). We will call the upper classes – in general the most wealthy – 'the élite', without giving this term any sentimental or moral significance. When the balance of social forces is stable, the members of this élite hold on to power, of which they can be assured, owing to their good or bad qualities.

But here an extremely important factor comes into play: aristocracies, or élites, do not last for long. Their descendants go into rapid decline, even those who are members of the élite because of nomination rather than heredity. This has been seen in all known communities. This is why the élite must perpetually replenish itself by drawing on the contribution of the lower classes: one can observe very clearly a movement which is the *circulation of élites*. Pareto carefully describes this with the help of many concrete facts and some very interesting historical observations (*Systèmes socialistes*, I. 42ff.; *Sociologie*, ch. XIII, passim). As with all other social phenomena, this movement does not occur with any regularity. 'A simple slowdown of this process could considerably increase the number of degenerative elements in the classes which still hold power, and conversely increase the superior elements in the lower classes. In this case, the balance of social forces becomes unstable.' The decadence of the élite becomes apparent in a growth of feeble humanitarianism, whilst a new élite full of strength and vigour arises in the inferior classes. 'Any élite which is not prepared to enter into battle to defend its position has fallen into decadence. There is nothing left for it, but to give way to another élite, which has the virile qualities that it lacks' (I. 40).

But this competition between two aristocracies is obscured by several factors. Because the movement is quite slow, its general tendency can only be observed over long periods of time, whereas the contemporary observer is given to taking the structure for the substance: 'He sees rivalries between

castes, oppression by a tyrant, popular uprisings, liberal demands, aristocracies, theocracies, mob rule by the worst elements' (I, 35). Such an
observer fails to detect the general phenomenon of which these are the
specific manifestations.

Furthermore, the new élite, to achieve its ends,[7] uses the lower class and
adopts its demands in order to gain power. 'The majority of historians do
not recognise this movement. They describe the phenomenon as if it were
the struggle of an aristocracy, always the same, against the people, always
the same' (I, 36). In fact, there are two aristocracies struggling for power,
and the composition of the aristocracy undergoes a constant process of
renewal.

The current phenomenon of socialism can, in fact, be explained by these
observations. Nowadays, socialists correctly emphasise the fact that the
revolutions which have occurred since 1789 have replaced the former aristocracy with the bourgeoisie. They sincerely believe that the future revolution will not have this outcome, and that a new élite of politicians will keep
their promises. In other words, it is always the future revolution which will
bring about the ultimate liberation of the lower classes. Unfortunately, for
centuries and centuries, the achievements of revolutions have become dis-
sipated at the very moment when they are thought to be reached. We now
know the true nature of this phenomenon.

At the present time, the governing class, made up principally of the
bourgeoisie and the remnants of the former aristocracy, proves every day
to be less able to defend its position, even though its aspirations are not
diminished. On the other hand, one can see the growth of a new aristocracy. Writing at the end of the nineteenth century, Pareto believed that the
leaders of the English trade unions, in particular, would take hold of
power and penetrate the upper class. One could observe in many places
the emergence of this new élite, which was energetic and decisive. What
would be the outcome of the struggle? Given a courageous army, full of
self-confidence, faced by timid, enervated troops, which grew weaker
every day through desertions, which side, asked Pareto, would you expect
to be victorious?[8]

We will not examine this question in any greater depth, as we will take it
up again in Chapter 6. The reader will now be in a position to understand
Pareto's work concerning socialism. It is profound and important, and one
can only regret that he did not write it in a more accessible style. As soon as
one has grasped the main line of thought in *Systèmes socialistes*, the book's
inner unity becomes clear. The basic division between social realities and
the logical value of ideas, described by Pareto, shows the true nature of

social phenomena and the insubstantiality of socialist arguments. These two sides of socialism are entirely separate. The theory, the doctrine, the way of reasoning, socialist derivations – these have no logico-experimental value, or very little. But, if we cease to concentrate on these things, we will discover behind them unchanging social phenomena and will come to recognise, at least in part, some of the major forces which influence society. Thus *Systèmes socialistes* is both a precursor to and a preparation for the *Trattato di sociologia generale*. The important theories in the latter book are found in embryonic form in the *Systèmes*, and the fundamental distinction on which they are based also forms the basis of the *Trattato*. Having already considered the derivations in chapter II,[9] we will now go on to Pareto's more specifically sociological work. We will, in particular, study the factors which determine social equilibrium.

5 The Sociologist

Georges H. Bousquet

It was the urge to add an indispensable extension to the study of political economy, and above all the inspiring example of natural sciences, which led me to write my Traité de sociologie, *of which the sole aim – I say sole, and I insist on this point – was to research into experimental reality by applying to the social sciences methods which have proved their worth in the fields of physics, chemistry, astronomy, biology and other similar sciences.*

Pareto, at his Jubilee

Pareto's sociological system was based on his economic system. He was always very clear about this point. In his *Cours [d'économie politique]*, he insisted that in a synthesis of concrete economic phenomena it was essential to take social factors into account, and stressed even more the inter-dependency of social relations. But, at the time, he was still not in a position to formulate theories for these relations and general social phenomena.

Therefore, since Pareto, before becoming a sociologist, was an economist and follower of Walras, it is necessary in order to understand his sociology, to understand the evolution of economic theory during the nineteenth century, an evolution which led to the theory of equilibrium. What had the classical economists done? Out of the immense number of premises which are to be found in society, they had illuminated human economic behaviour, and had abstracted it from the rest of social reality. They worked on this basis either by analysing the facts, or by trying – with a new abstraction – to construct theories on this basis, that is to say, to place them within a framework which would provide a general overview.

Thus, the classical economists had discovered a series of theories which were to a certain extent all related with each other, but also had a certain independence: the theories of rent, production, wages, price determination, 'value', etc. Towards the middle of the last century, economists had in this way succeeded in creating a coherent whole. The study of economics was believed to be all but complete, at the very moment when the subject was going to expand again, thanks to Gossen, Menger, Jevons, Walras, and others.

We have seen how Walras brought together all the known economic theory of his age in a grandiose synthesis, by completing and even elaborating this theory, using his system of economic equilibrium, which was then taken up by his successor Pareto. But then Pareto hit upon this brilliant idea: would it not be possible to do for sociology what the great Walras had done for economics? Could a theory be constructed which would give us an approximate idea of the structure of human society? This idea is the point of departure for an understanding of his sociology.

It is well to imagine what courage was needed to consider such a line of thought. An initial obstacle was the predominant attitude amongst the educated public towards social studies. Then, definite knowledge in the field of social studies was a lot less advanced when Pareto started his work than when Walras formulated his theory of equilibrium. Finally, such a project would demand a considerable amount of money, personal contacts and 'deductive energy'.

However, he set to work and thanks to his twenty years of practical and theoretical knowledge, thanks to his mind, equally gifted in the field of mathematics, philology and history, thanks to a further twenty years of work, he wrote his *Sociologie* (or *Trattato*).

I

Pareto's approach to social realities is not lacking in eloquence, and the influence of pure economics can be clearly seen. The latter uses the idea of *Homo œconomicus* who acts logically, that is to say that any other acts are not taken into account. *Homo œconomicus* or, if you prefer, Man, when considered in terms of economics, bases his actions on observation or experience, from which by objective and logical deductions he draws precise conclusions. It was necessary, then, to discover whether this hypothesis of logical behaviour was generally substantiated by the behaviour of Man in society and if not, to find some other hypothesis which took account of the facts.

For example, an American banker observed that at certain periods the rate of exchange in New York compared to London was high, whereas regularly at other times, as a result of payments in reverse, the opposite was true. Following a series of logical deductions, he was led to buy against the London rate of exchange in the latter period in order to sell later, which was a logical and experimental act.

This observation, Pareto says, demonstrates that a large number of human actions belong in this category, as much in economics as in technology, law, strategy, and so on. But there are still other factors. This same banker may refuse to sit down to a meal with twelve other people, or with a Negro or a Japanese man. If he is a Catholic, he will perform some ritual so that one of his children will be restored to health. He may observe masonic ritual. He may give way to expressions of enthusiasm if he sees the president pass, or take his hat off before the Stars and Stripes. The characteristic of all these actions, is that they are not – to the observer – the objective result of experimental deduction or of a logical theory. We will define them (in other words, we choose to call them, says Pareto), as non-logical actions. But one could call them X actions or something else.

This X actions theory should have two aims: firstly, it is necessary to see whether one can reduce them to a general pattern, similar to that in Gossen's law; secondly, it must be shown that our concept of X actions is useful in our aim of understanding the general structure of societies: in order to do that, it must be shown that, in a social context, the majority of people's actions belong to the X type of actions. If logical actions are largely the result of reasoning, then non-logical actions derive mainly from a certain state of mind.

Pareto used the inductive method to study the nature of these actions. He attempted to identify the constant and the variable factors. To this end, he studied a particular case in detail: the non-logical actions which were designed to call up or ward off storms, actions which have lasted to the present day. He also drew a parallel between the histories of Rome and Athens to discover more about these non-logical actions, their importance and their different characteristics in the two cities. In short, he was led to believe that the constant factors in human behaviour consisted of certain sentiments which had existed from time immemorial to the present day; with regard to variable factors, there were more or less logical explanations, theoretical proofs which he aimed to give.

Instead of the large quantity of proofs given in *Sociologie,* I will give a single contemporary example to explain the theory of non-logical action (*S.* 80). In 1923 Lord Carnarvon, who led the archaeological dig at the tomb of the pharaoh Tutankhamun, died in circumstances said to be 'mysterious'. At the time, the idea of a 'posthumous revenge' by the pharaoh caught many people's imagination. If the reader will recall the absurdities which were uttered over this episode by spiritists, magi, clairvoyants, theosophists, he will remember that every explanation was different: I remember having read that it was a matter of the 'astral double' of the deceased, or a certain subtle poison, or even the 'reincarnation' of the pharaoh in the form of a venomous insect. The idea that the violation of the tomb demanded revenge was the main point. The public did not accept this theory by following a logico-experimental deduction. On the contrary, it was the confused sentiments surrounding this revenge which led some people to accept the theory and others to formulate it. If we analyse these sentiments, we will find at least three different elements in them: (a) the confused notion of a dead person having a continued relation with the things that belonged to him during his life; (b) the idea that certain objects have a mysterious influence when combined in a certain way; (c) the feeling that a particular order of things had been changed, that the dead person's integrity had been violated, and that there were certain ways of restoring that integrity. The fact which is of great interest is that these sentiments are not isolated or unusual, but are the basis of countless human customs, manifesting themselves in speech and action.

In fact, Pareto analyses and classifies both human behaviour and human reasoning. With regard to both, he arrives at the same conclusion: man in society performs non-logical acts (not to be mistaken for 'illogical') which he claims to justify with imprecise arguments, and which are based on certain instincts, on certain invariable sentiments. Conversely, man constructs or accepts non-logico-experimental theories and doctrines, because they embody certain psychological tendencies. Pareto identifies two elements in theories and verbal phenomena, and refers to them by single letters of the alphabet, in order to base his argument on facts rather than words. 'Concerning concrete theories, which we will refer to as (c), behind factual postulates, there are two basic elements, the first of which we will refer to as (a), and a contingent and generally variable element, which we will refer to as (b). Part (a) is directly related to non-logical actions, and expresses certain sentiments. Part (b) is the expression of man's need for (pseudo) logic. People are clearly most influenced by the main part of the phenomenon, and subsequently try to justify it. It is part (a) that is the main part, and consequently this part is the most important for research into social equilibrium' (*S*. 798, 800).

In this classification of social factors, Pareto, following the method used in other sciences, tries to separate invariable from variable phenomena. What *remain*, what are invariable, are certain tendencies, certain sentiments; let us call them (says Pareto) '*residues*'. The things that vary are arguments, theories, nomenclature, that *derive* from this state of mind; let us call them (he says), '*derivations*'. It was in this way that Pareto formulated the idea of derivation which we have already studied in chapter II,[1] and which he ana-lysed in psychological and logical terms in his *Sociologie*. The reader will now understand the close connection between Pareto's sociological system and his logical system. This is the idea that Man is not a logical animal, sentiments constituting an essential part of his nature.

II

These few inferences are not sufficient from a scientific point of view to support the theory of non-logical actions. A scientific theory is only valid in so far as it can be verified experimentally. A third of *Sociologie* is devoted to the classification of residues and derivations, with such an abundance of detail, such a wealth of concrete facts, that one forgets the purely deductive goal that the author is aiming at. In fact, this goal is not of great importance. The whole of this part of the work is extremely evocative in itself. Pareto vividly illuminates the nature of social phenomena, revealing their true nature to us.

We shall discuss here only residues, since the classification of derivations has already been mentioned. Actually, I understand from the author himself that the classification of residues should be seen as provisional, and will quite soon be out of date. But science can make use of all 'useful' or 'convenient' means for understanding reality. This classification can be kept as a scientific method, at least provisionally.

First Class: The instinct for combinations[2]

According to Pareto, this is one of the instincts which have contributed most to the development of civilisation. Many logical things that we do today derive from or correspond to non-logical combinations of the past. The scientist combines certain elements in his laboratory, in much the same way as a child amuses himself putting different things together or the savage carries out magical practices. In general terms, this residue explains a great many non-logical actions. It goes without saying that the 'residue' is only an abstract idea; a concrete phenomenon is made up of numerous elements which we analyse separately. Combinations can occur by chance, or according to certain non-logico-experimental laws. Thus the similarity or dissimilarity of things is a powerful cause of combinations. They are found in magical practices, when it was believed for example that one could influence a person, an animal or an object by working on a part which had been taken from them. Also the basic principles of *similia similibus* and *contraria contraribus curantur* (like cures like, opposites are cured by opposites) reveal this kind of residue. People also readily make a connection between different exceptional occurrences; it is this that explains the divine origin assigned to heroes and great men, as well as the belief in omens. Pareto recalls the premonitions of Nero's death, as related by Suetonius: 'These investigations', says he, 'are similar to those of our theologians and metaphysicians today. One gets out of them exactly what one has put in. Why should the fact that a mule gives birth foreshadow some important event? One cannot find any other explanation than the coincidence of a rare event with another rare event which the Romans thought must be disastrous' (S. 925). Often men have believed that by assimilating certain things, they would in part take on the characteristics of these things. This non-logical belief belongs in the first class, and explains numerous social phenomena from totems to various religious practices. As always, the derivations are variable, but the foundation of residues hardly changes at all.

Very often, certain objects or actions are invested with a mysterious power. 'One finds this residue in many magical practices, in amulets, oaths made over certain things, ordeals, etc. It is also the main part of taboos, with or without penalties' (*S.* 944). The ideas about religious relics reveal a similar sentiment; magical practices also give rise to a great number of mysterious acts.

At this point Pareto carefully analyses the theories about perfect numbers: 'They clearly show the difference between the logico-experimental thinking and that governed by sentiments. For mathematicians, *perfect* is just a label used to indicate a number equal to the sum of its even parts.... One could use some other term, for example one could call them *imperfect*, but nothing, absolutely nothing, would have changed... Things are very different when sentiments control thought. The name then becomes highly important: *perfect* is the opposite of *imperfect* and the grounds for including a number among those which are perfect would be the same as those for removing it from those which are imperfect. Furthermore, one does not know the precise meaning of the word perfect any more than one knows the meaning of similar terms, such as right, good, true, beautiful. It just seems that these words are epithets for certain agreeable sentiments, felt by certain people' (*S.* 960).

Pareto cites the followers of Pythagoras, and then Saint Augustine: 'According to logico-experimental deduction, it would be ridiculous to state: Six is equal to the sum of its factors, therefore God must have created the world in six days'. There is no connection between the premise and the con-clusion. But, conversely, thought based on sentiment makes this connection, thanks to the word *perfect*, which is then, over time, no longer mentioned in this context; this is a common process. It may seem that we have spoken too extensively of these odd ideas, and this might be so if one wanted to consider them from a logico-experimental point of view. But if they are considered from a subjective point of view, noticing that they have been held by an immense number of people at all times, it becomes clear that they must correspond to widespread and powerful sentiments which, consequently, cannot be neglected in a study of social structures' (*S.* 963, 964).

Generally speaking, the residues of the first class are related to the fashion for novelty and change. However, they make for great social stability when they are joined to the residues of the second class.

Second Class: Prevalence of aggregations

This is one of the most interesting psychological theories. Pareto shows that in the human mind certain aggregations of sentiments, certain groups of psychological complexes develop, and subsequently, for the individual, assume an objective reality. This persistence of collectivities is a much more powerful spur to action than theories or even realities. Thus there is not a 'thing' called a 'country' in the same sense that there is a 'thing' called 'umbrella' or an animal called 'elephant'. No objective reality outside the individual corresponds to this term. But the sentiment of patriotism is one of the most important social factors. It shows people's continual affinity with places, with men of past ages, and so on. Also belonging in this class are sentiments connected with religion, the family, social classes – in the sense of castes and sects, – sentiments which are basic to the worship of ancestors, and, finally, all the sentiments which people transform into objective realities (Progress, Democracy, Socialism, Nationalism, Justice, Beauty, etc.). All these words denote groups of sentiments which are very strong, but not clearly defined. Although they have no objective reality, it is necessary, in order to understand them, to take into account the fact that people believe they have.

These residues are related to 'religious' sentiments, taking this term in its broadest sense. Again, numerous examples demonstrate that the variable appearance of the derivations conceals residues that hardly alter.

Third Class: The need to show one's sentiments by outward actions

One can make the same observation with regard to the residues of the third class. A particularly striking example is that of religious ecstasy, since its characteristics have been practically the same in all countries, at all times. But theological derivations have nothing in common with each other.

Fourth Class: Sentiments related to sociability

It is these which explain the growth of certain associations and the need for
uniformity. This need is shown by the important role played by conformity
in society. 'The residue is shown in an almost pure form in the way fashion
imposes transient uniformity.... Not only do people conform in order to look
like other people, they also want others to do the same. If someone appears
in a different style, this gives rise, irrationally, to a feeling of uneasiness
amongst the people who are with him or her. They try to erase the difference
by persuasion, or more often disapprobation, or – even more often – force.
As usual, there is no lack of empty logical perorations to explain this
attitude. But the real reason is not to be found among them. The reason, at
least to a large extent, is the feelings of hostility against violations of
uniformity' (*S.* 1126). There is little point in citing examples, since there is
an abundance of them. Also included in this class are: neophobia, pity,
cruelty, hierarchical attitudes, and finally asceticism, in relation to which
Pareto, with some pleasure, dwells on the history of flagellation.

**Fifth Class: Integrity of the individual and the appurtenances he
relies on**

It must be noted that there are two types of important sentiments in this
class. In the first place, there are those which are related to the purification
rites so common in primitive societies, and which are still found today
amongst savage people, in a number of religious ceremonies amongst
civilised societies, and even (*P.* 115n.) in non-religious ceremonies. All
these actions have given rise to a great proliferation of derivations. The
other residue, which is perhaps even more important, is the 'sentiment
which dislikes changes in the social equilibrium'. People living in society
formulate a certain ideal of social relations and if this happens to be altered,
they suffer because of this alteration, even if it does not harm them directly.
If this sentiment did not exist, every change caused by a weak social
equilibrium would meet very little opposition, or none at all. Consequently,
the transformation would be able to continue unchecked, until it affected a
sufficiently large number of individuals to cause resistance by those
wanting to directly prevent the damage... By adding to the residue under
consideration the first class residues, one could form combined residues of
great social importance, corresponding to vivid and powerful sentiments,
similar to those which, with very little precision, are referred to by the term
'ideal of justice'. From a logico-experimental point of view, to say that the

'injustice' committed against a single person is an offence against 'justice' as great as that committed against a large number of people does not make sense. 'There is no one person who bears the name "justice" and we do not know which offences could be committed against it.' But the residue which is embodied in this derivation is useful to society (1216). It is because of this residue, not the theories of the philosophers who perorate about 'justice' that society reaches stability.

Sixth Class: Sexual residue:

There is no need to show the persistence of this residue from ancient times to the present day. But Pareto, who was a major critic[3] of the hypocrisy of our ways – hypocrisy which, before the war, had spread from the Germanic and Anglo-Saxon countries to the Latin ones – demonstrates that, most often, acts of 'virtuism', which hope to suppress any signs of people's sexual impulse, are themselves a hidden expression of the sexual impulse.

Such, then, is Pareto's theory of residues. It brings us to the following conclusion: non-logical actions make up the greatest part of individual actions in society. Thus, in theorising about them, we are able to understand the general structure of society. It is necessary to see two separate elements in actions: the first element has remained more or less constant throughout the centuries, namely, a certain state of mind made up of various sentiments; the second is a variable element, seen in 'explanations', theories, and pseudo-logical justifications, in short, all the ways in which people make use of language. Therefore, contrary to what one would normally believe, people do not act under the influence of certain theories, but they have a certain state of mind which, on the one hand, impels them to act, and on the other, makes them look for theories, for supposedly logical 'explanations' of their behaviour.[4]

But if this a quite normal development in society, how is it that social theorists are still not aware of the fact? Pareto shows that the phenomenon had already been partly understood, but had not been accepted as a general theory, because it was much more easy to believe that people behaved logically, as suggested by the derivations, than to look objectively for the truth. If one examines these ideas, one sees that most often their originators take as their point of departure their own sentiments, instead of basing their argument on objective observation and experience: 'There are very few authors who totally fail to consider non-logical actions. They generally appear in the study of certain natural tendencies that the author recognises. But these tendencies are reduced to a minimum, and it is assumed that men draw logical conclusions from them, and act accordingly' (261). Pareto backs up his assertion by his critique of Aristotle, Plato, Saint Thomas, Comte, Mill, Spencer, Condorcet and others. In brief, he formulated 'a theory, whose many strands are scattered in such a way as to make them barely recognizable' (842). We will now consider the corollaries of this theory.

III

An analysis of the facts thus allows us to isolate certain abstract elements in actual phenomena, which is an approach similar to that used in pure economics. This approach leads to a better understanding of the nature of social phenomena. The last three chapters of *Sociologie* are devoted to this end. Since their author always uses the same 'method of exposition', we are forced to consider the subject in a slightly different fashion, and the division which we will make bears no relation to that contained in the work itself.

In the first instance, Pareto examines certain questions concerning the deductive system that he wished to construct. Before this point, he had not taken account of the relative number of social phenomena displaying different residues. An observation of the facts – to which Pareto makes copious references – allows us to draw the following conclusion: derivations are highly variable. If we ignore them, we will be able to find quite marked variations in each type of residue, which would correspond to a given class for each one; whereas a class of residues, taken as a whole, shows little or no variation over time, when a society is considered as a whole. It is necessary to understand this in terms of averages, since there is a series of undulations which fluctuate about a median line. Furthermore, though certain classes of residues may be more or less constant in the same society, their significance can vary greatly from one society to another, and they can show great disparities in the various social strata (*P.* 123, 124).

Regarding the spread of residues to other places, it is difficult to tell whether this is because of simple imitation or is the product of certain circumstances which come into play first in one place, and then in another. The latter case is the most common, since one can observe the modification of combined residues together with political and economic changes...Conversely, derivations are disseminated above all by imitation; at certain periods, theological derivations are in fashion, at other metaphysical derivations, and so on.

Until now, we have taken the residues to be the cause and the derivations to be the effect. This viewpoint reflects the general way of things, but we should not forget the interrelatedness of all social phenomena. In general, a derivation is not accepted because it has logical value, but because it is a clear expression of the sentiments which many people vaguely feel. This is the primary phenomenon. But the fact of its general acceptance causes the derivation to increase the power and vigour of the sentiments which it expresses. This is the secondary phenomenon.

Pareto then studied several examples of 'virtual movements', as one puts it in engineering terminology. He looked into the effects the governing authority could achieve by trying to suppress or change certain residues or derivations in a given society. His conclusion underlines the great difficulty in modifying residues and consequently the obstacles which obstruct the introduction of new laws.

Taken as a whole, these analyses led Pareto to make the following propositions: it is commonly said that 'fervent derivations are more success-ful in inciting men to act than cold rationality. One can accept this elliptical mode of expression, provided that one makes it clear that it is not a question of derivations, but rather of the sentiments which they manifest. Sentiments expressed by derivations which go beyond experience and reality are very effective in leading men to action. This fact explains very clearly the phe-nomenon observed and illuminated by Georges Sorel: that successful social doctrines (or, more correctly, the sentiments displayed in these doctrines) assume the form of myths. To express differently an observation which has been made so many times before, we will say that the social value of these doctrines – or the sentiments which they express – should not be judged by their mythical form, which is only a mode of behaviour, but essentially by the end result' (*S.* 1867–8). Pareto then formulates a complete theory of social myths, making a clear distinction between the idealised objectives and the actual achievements of society. He also explains why myths have usually benefited societies, though this is not necessarily so (1874, 1875). This leads him to analyse at length the derivations on these matters uttered by moralists, political philosophers, etc. (1876–2002). At this point, we come across a new theory, that of social utility, but it is so abstract and diffi-cult, that we can only indicate what the author intended to achieve. Ordi-narily, people do not agree about what is 'useful' to society. Pareto shows that these disagreements are most often quibbles (derivations) because people confuse two things: the means of achieving a goal, and the goal itself. A discussion about the first of these – the means – can be objective, but one about the second – the goal – cannot, since it is not for science to determine whether the ideal for society should be X, Y, or Z. Following on from this statement, he then formulates a strictly scientific language in order to study these questions. He insists upon the need to make a distinction between two utility optima for societies, a distinction which again derives from pure economics. The latter serves to underpin sociological thought, to give it some sort of direction in these extraordinarily complex enquiries.

Pareto states that it is crucial to recognise that one can attribute any kind of goal to society, and pronounce it to be 'useful', but this usefulness has nothing in common with the utility one would arrive at by adding up all the utilities of the members of society, such a total being impossible to arrive at, given that there are a number of 'ophelimities' relating to different subjects. One could only arrive at such a figure by means of arbitrary conventions. The admirer of the superhuman would rate the usefulness of the lower classes as almost nothing; the democrat would accord them a higher coefficient. Science would have nothing to say on this matter. When we have fully understood this highly abstract theory of 'social utility' we can again see the futility of an infinite number of derivations.

At this point, Pareto had achieved his aim. He had unified all of his research in a synthesis, which gives us in an initial and rough aproximation, a general idea of the actual structure of society. We will not concern ourselves here with the formulas he used (*P.* 142f). They deal with society's structure and its 'utility'; and it is clear that these are mainly determined by the equilibrium of residues and not by the conflict of derivations. I would only ask the reader to consider the precise nature of the theories to which we are referring here; they are analogous to the theories of pure economics, and, in short, from the *Cours* to *Sociologie*, Pareto alone developed a scientific approach that can be compared to the change from the preclassical economics of the eighteenth century to Walras's work on the equilibrium of exchange published in August 1873.[5]

IV

But the *Sociologie* contains many other things, since, while pursuing his main theme, Pareto tackles a number of interesting subjects about which we ought to say a few words.

One thing he looks at (*S.* 1755–1760) is the role of the major daily newspapers and the way they influence the public.

The indeterminate nature of derivations, especially religious derivations, leads him to enquire into how they can be modified for certain ends. Pareto then recounts the history of the Franciscans and the policies of the Popes towards them: 'The mentality of the Popes with regard to the Franciscan phenomenon depended on various causal factors... in the main, residues from the first class operated [upon them] and the Popes had to resolve the problem which governing powers often have to face: to know how, by means of favourable alliances, to make use of sentiments which could produce adversaries, or favour existing adversaries, in order to fight these same adversaries. The waves of religiosity and superstition rose up over the papal bulwarks. The Pope called upon the very same religiosity and superstition to provide the means of reinforcing this bulwark. This is why if we glance only casually at papal measures concerning the Franciscans, they seem changing and contradictory; but if, on the contrary, we go to the heart of the matter, leaving out exceptional cases such as that of Celestin V, they seem perfectly unified and leading up to a single goal' (*S*.1810). Of course, it was here that derivations really came into their own, as Pareto demonstrates in a detailed history.

Elsewhere (2156f) he devotes about ten pages to historiography. He contrasts philosophical, theological and political history with scientific history, which must be more concerned with residues than with derivations. For example, Augustus was condemned for having founded the Empire, when he had claimed he would restore the Republic; likewise Robespierre, an opponent of the death penalty, for having used it. These ethical judge-ments are without interest. Conversely, in a scientific approach, there are two problems to be resolved. The first is not of major importance, that of the good or bad character of these people. 'The second question, which, almost uniquely, has any bearing on history, is to discover how and why the sentiments and interests embodied in these derivations achieved success. Can one really believe that the Romans were misled by Augustus, and the French by Robespierre? This thesis is untenable.' In fact, even the personalities of Augustus and Robespierre are not all that significant and the true problem is as follows: why did the sentiments and interests personified by these men prevail over the sentiments and interests personified by their enemies? Among all the casual factors, derivations played only a minor second role.

Immediately afterwards, Pareto considers an important problem: the use of force in society. He approaches this in his usual way: he considers the prob-lem in its concrete and objective aspects and compares it with the derivations arising from it. Here, he touches upon the difference between governments which mainly use guile (residues of the first class) and those using force (res-idues of the second class) to stay in power. He formulates the complete the-ory a little later on, when he studies different political regimes: the actual

manner in which they govern, he says, is much the same; it is their appearance which above all seems different. It is always a minority which holds
power. Political parties are also analysed at this point.

Pareto is interested in many other phenomena. He makes a distinction
between two classes of 'capitalists' which is very important from a
sociological viewpoint. There were, he said, those who had fixed incomes
and those whose incomes varied according to their abilities and the general
economic situation. These two classes of people had divergent interests,
often conflicting, more conflicting even than the interests of the business
and working classes.[6]

This would explain many social phenomena. This economic difference,
says Pareto, conceals another deeper one, a psychological difference.
Amongst those with fixed incomes (called R) there is an overriding desire for
stability and, in general, second class residues predominate. Amongst those
whose incomes are variable (called S), there is a liking for networking, and, in
general, a predominance of first class residues. Thanks to the R group,
societies can become stable, while members of category S bring about change
and economic development.[7]

R people play another very important role, that of supplying capital to
society from their savings. A simple examination of the facts will show that
they are continuously stripped of their assets over the course of time.
Pareto provides an incredible amount of historical evidence regarding this.
His overall conclusion is that private property can only exist in society at
the price of continual assaults.

V

In this long exposition, Pareto often studies the shape taken by social
phenomena over the course of time. He is always forced to the same
conclusion: the different factors of social life show a continuous series of
oscillations, of undulations whose periods are highly variable: small,
medium or large. Throughout the ages, moreover, people had a vague
conception of this rhythmic, periodic, oscillating, undulating aspect of social
phenomena. It was only when, Pareto noted, one wanted to construct a theory
from this, that writers were bogged down in metaphysical speculations (Vico,
Ferrari, and others). In any case, 'if one looks at all these phenomena from a
distance, and sees that they have been occurring and recurring at regular
intervals from time immemorial to the present day, it is impossible not to
admit that the observed oscillations are the rule, and that they are not about to

cease. As to what will happen in the far and distant future, we do not know. But it is very likely that the course of events, already so extended, is not able to change direction in the near future' (*S.* 2391).

But would it not be possible to construct a scientific theory of social cycles? Pareto answered that it would be, and indeed, we have not yet reached the end of the *General Sociology*. This time, Pareto took sociology beyond the boundaries that neither he nor Walras were able to cross in pure economics: passing from the static to the dynamic. In fact, the studies which he undertook henceforward did not produce any theoretical formulas. They remained inductive, but nevertheless the influence of pure economics was strongly in evidence.

The basic idea behind this dynamic is that all the elements of social evolution are interdependent. Until now, we have seen attempts at causal explanation. For example, social phenomena have been ascribed a single cause, whether an imaginary cause (Bossuet's will of God) or a concrete cause (Marx's economic materialism). However, an analysis of the facts proves that this was an error similar to that made by economists who sought (and still seek!) to discover a single cause determining value, whereas this economic quantity is not just an effect, but also a cause of the things that determine it. In the same way, it cannot be argued that economic evolution is the *cause* of social evolution, because a given factor of social evolution (residues, for example) determines economic evolution in a different way. In other words, the two factors form an equilibrium, mutually determining each other.

It is impossible for us to consider all the factors of social evolution. We must start by studying some of the most important ones, with a more detailed study later on. Thus, Pareto only considers four factors: interest (the economic phenomenon), residues (the psychological phenomenon), derivations (ideology), and finally, the circulation of élites, a phenomenon which originates in social heterogeneity, the theory of which was the basis of the *Systèmes socialistes* as we have seen.

Thus, social evolution is a series of interdependent cycles. But at this point a difficulty occurs. In order to consider this mutual dependence, it is necessary to use mathematical terms, which alone can clearly describe this kind of relationship. Such terms are, however, irrelevant to sociology. It is necessary, therefore, to examine the relationship of cause and effect, at the same time taking into account their dependence on each other and considering consecutive actions and reactions. The mathematical processes used in pure economics are useful as a guide here, and show in plain terms the mistakes to be avoided (*S.* 1732).

Using these important ideas, Pareto delineates the broad sweep of social evolution in different societies. His method was to use a series of approximations, often returning to the same theme. He carefully shows the action that each of the aforementioned factors has on the others and the consequent reaction. Together, these actions and reactions determine the shape of the cycle, which always has a limited duration. As one might expect, the influence of derivations on residues, on the circulation of élites and on the economic phenomenon is weak. Conversely, derivations themselves are strongly influenced by these three factors. This section of the book is highly interesting, opening new horizons.

VI

We will now attempt to make an overall assessment of Pareto's sociological system.

Those who have fully understood the essence of the *Trattato di sociologia generale* find that the overall impression it makes on them leads them to admire the inspired character of its author, indeed the term 'inspired' seems inadequate as a description of Pareto. At his jubilee at Lausanne, Professor Pantaleoni expressed veneration for him. Truly, one can think of few men whose scientific approach has been as far-reaching as that of Pareto. One can only echo the views of Professor Guido Sensini, who said: 'I do not know whether literature anywhere in the world embraces another work, in whatever genre, which for variety of material, interpretive genius, or meticulousness of the logico-experimental research method, can be compared with the *Trattato*.'[8]

In line with Pareto's own method, however, we would not be able to make an assessment of the whole of his system, without analysing its various parts as well. I will not consider the theory of derivations in so far as it constitutes a new form of logic. In his book, Pareto did not clearly distinguish between the sociological and logical aspects of derivation, but it was necessary to do this in order to demonstrate the manifold aspects of his work. The theory of derivations by itself would be enough to establish a man's reputation. Was Pareto equally successful when he formulated a positivist doctrine?

To give an opinion on the question, it should be remembered that science is only made up of a series of approximations. His theories are merely a way of helping us understand reality. This being so, one can state that Pareto gave us a series of extremely powerful configurations as a means of grasping reality but without aiming at an exact representation, which would diminish their value.

The theories of non-logical action and residues are examples of this. They allow us to see a link between many facts which seemed not to have anything in common. Besides, they originate in pure economics, which has successfully used abstract methods. Consequently, it is necessary to make the fullest use of them. It is an undeniable fact, as Pareto demonstrated, that alongside logical actions people perform these other, non-logical, actions. But it is less easy for sociologists to concede the importance of residues. To want to identify, even abstractly, in a social phenomenon or an individual action, a combination of *n* residues in different proportions, in each one seeing various classes and sub-classes, will seem offensive to many intellectuals. In order to defend Pareto's viewpoint, however, one can turn to a fact referred to by Hans Vaihinger in his *Philosophie des Als-Ob*. In science, he says, one either finds *hypotheses*, which it should be possible to verify by future experiments, or *fictions*, which though known to be inexact, are adopted simply because they are convenient notions. Therefore, the hypothesis-residue should be discarded, whereas the fiction-residue should be kept. Pareto himself was of much the same view, as well as the great chemist Berthollet, who studying the calorie hypothesis,[9] ended up saying the same thing: 'One must admit that the hypothesis [we will say: the fiction] does no harm and is useful in that it uses only general and invariable principles to explain phenomena.' Thus, he adopted the attitude which is typical in science and modern philosophy. We cannot do better than to adopt the same attitude when considering the 'fiction' of the residue, and in so doing, we will not forgo the option of discarding this notion in the future. In a previous chapter, we saw how Pareto himself removed a similar 'fiction' from pure economics, the quantification of pleasure. Perhaps a way will also be found of substituting another theory for the residue, which we have to keep for the moment.

We can summarise this by stating that the idea of residues is at least as useful for sociology as the idea of ultimate utility has been as a means of understanding economic phenomena, which is equally approximate. But, as we know, Pareto went on to use the idea of residues as a means of deduction, in order to arrive at a system of pure sociology. In contrast to former approaches to sociology, which were far removed from reality, this system had as its aim the representation of social reality, in the same way that the concept of economic equilibrium provided a picture of economic reality. Also, when we consider that the system is not fully developed, and that the research which led to its formulation (residues and derivations) constitutes a far greater achievement than the finished work, it is only appropriate to admire what depth of insight Pareto achieved and to realise what a gargantuan task he undertook. That the approach to human understanding of certain problems took such a great leap forward in such a short space of time is, in my view, a unique occurrence in the history of science. Pareto wanted to formulate an all-embracing theory in a science which some people said had not yet begun. Around the age of forty, he still saw society only as an arena for his practical activity. Later on, he started to study it using method akin to theoretical physics. One could perhaps cite instances of changes which were similarly rapid, in the history of literature, science, the arts, etc., but these changes would be those resulting from the work of several generations of thinkers. That such an advance was the work of a single thinker is almost incomprehensible.[10] But, having said this, there are perhaps a few reservations to be made about Pareto's actual legacy in this area. Possibly the evidence behind his arguments, so remarkable in the other sections of the *Sociologie*, once one has understood the ideas of the author, does not carry so much weight in his theory of equilibrium. That this theory is extremely interesting is indisputable; that its terminology helps us to understand the facts, we must admit; that thanks to this approach we are able to take our studies much further is clear. But we must not be afraid to state that, as an objective body, his theories can in no way be compared to the work of Walras. Walras's scientific ideal went far beyond that of Pareto. With regard to their comparative theories of social and economic equilibrium, Walras built a far more solid structure than his successor. We have already underlined the fact that the theory of economic equilibrium did not represent a faithful picture of reality; all the more reason then for this to be said of the idea of social equilibrium. It is not clear, given our present level of understanding, how it could be directly applied to the facts. Shall I go further and state that the author himself had great difficulty in doing this? We should remember that Pareto spoke to us in terms of a mechanism of stable, unstable and dynamic states of equilibrium. If I might be allowed to inject a personal note, I would like to say that I had the honour to put a few specific questions to him on this matter. For example, I asked him what was the most appropriate category for the period called the Industrial Revolution in England, and it seemed to me that his answer was somewhat vague.[11] Poincaré speaks somewhere of principles born out of experience, but which experience can no longer even contradict. Perhaps we should put Pareto's system of static social equilibrium into a similar category.

We should adopt a very different opinion concerning his studies of social evolution which, moreover, are of a totally different type. The *circulation of élites* is a scientific theory, since it allows us to assemble in a 'convenient, useful' way many concrete facts. The major advantage of this dynamic is that it is based solely on observation, and above all, that it clearly unites the study of general sociology with that of economics. In particular, the natural analogy between major economic periods and social cycles is an important discovery. As regards the undulating pattern in social phenomina, its discovery rid us of a mass of erroneous theories. Moreover, a whole range of phenomena following on from the publication of the *Trattato* confirmed this pattern. However, in considering the essential character of this dynamic, there remains, in our view, one important observation to be made to which no one has yet given any thought. According to Pareto's way of thinking, the social dynamic remains static, by which I mean that it results from new combinations of similar elements, and that this is inevitable. Pareto insisted that he was trying to identify constant factors which lay behind an appearance of variability. But is it so certain that present-day societies only appear to be different from ancient societies? Is the 'concrete form', to quote Pareto, at root so similar? Has the author's method perhaps caused him to neglect the difference? The question will be resolved by posterity. It is enough for us to state that if these basic differences exist, Pareto could not have perceived them given the route he followed. This statement moreover does not make any assumptions in regard to the answer to the question put here.

These are some of the observations which we wanted to make before studying another aspect of Pareto's thought. His *Trattato* is in itself a masterpiece of the human intellect. Thanks to this work, the true structure of societies, hidden by countless derivations, starts to emerge. It will thus be interesting to see what conclusions, relating to the structure of present-day society, Pareto drew from his work. The next chapter will be devoted to this question.

6 Pareto and the Problems of Modern Society

Georges H. Bousquet

To compare our own times with the beginning of the nineteenth century would seem to be like comparing the dawn with the twilight, but in the end reality could be different from appearances.

Pareto

Pareto's ideas about modern society are found mainly in his *Sociologie*, but also in other publications, particularly his post-war articles. A remarkable note of scepticism, borne out of his sociological studies, is apparent. This attitude is interesting in itself. We do not propose to spend a great deal of time over it; it is indubitably a curious aspect of his thought, but Pareto's main work is to be found elsewhere.

I

It is certain that we have reached a situation that has close analogies with that in which the Roman plutocracy found itself at the end of the Republic.

Pareto (*Trattato* 86)

As we have seen, Pareto studied in his *Sociologie* the way in which important social factors are interdependent, namely, sentiments, derivations, economic matters and the circulation of élites. With the help of this research, he was able to outline the structure of modern western European society. The most important phenomenon was seen to be found in the interaction between economic prosperity and social heterogeneity. According to Pareto, one could initially study a limited cycle of interdependence, in which interests had an influence on the movement of élites and vice-versa: 'If one wanted to show briefly the differences between the social situation before the French Revolution and the current situation, one would say that they mainly consisted in a predominance of economic interests and a

greatly intensified mobility of élites. Except for a small number of obstacles, in Germany and Austria [1913], not only have all the hindrances to the
mobility of élites disappeared, but that phenomenon has grown in intensity,
owing to the support of economic prosperity' (*S.* 2300). In short, all those
who combine a large quantity of first-class residues with success in all
kinds of economic enterprises, are certain to become part of the ruling
class, along with other people who are equally characterised by an instinct
for combinations.

Pareto studied the psychological and economic characteristics of this
ruling class. He showed that as a whole they were favourable to the growth
of prosperity. In this, he could identify aspects of action and counteraction.
'When periods of rapid growth of economic prosperity are greater than
periods of economic stagnation, the ruling class always takes on more *S*
[see p.54 above] thereby reinforcing the instinct-combinations residues.
The *R*, people who generally embody residues favouring aggregations,
become less well represented among the ruling class, the altered composition of which encourages expanding participation in business enterprises
and increased prosperity, until such time as new forces emerge which
counter this tendency' (*S.* 2312). Pareto calls this the *cycle of demagogic
plutocracy*. He always maintained that this cycle, like any other historical
cycle, would not last indefinitely. He had already shown in his *Systèmes*
that certain forces militated against its perpetuity. By virtue of having
underlined these facts before the war, Pareto earned the title of the prophet
of Bolshevism and Fascism. Moreover, he was not satisfied simply to study
the limited cycle of interaction between social heterogeneity and economic
phenomena. He added to this a study of residues (*S.* 2321f.) and derivations. The influence of the cycle on derivations was remarkable: 'It is easy
to understand that derivations adapt to the new circumstances created by
the circulation of élites. They are affected, albeit to a small extent, by the
change in economic conditions. From this point of view, they can be seen
as the effects of these causes. As the dominant class grows rich in individuals in whom the instinct for combinations predominates, and as it feels
reluctant to use force openly, so derivations arise that are adapted to these
modes of thought. Humanitarianism and pacificism spring up and grow in
popularity. People talk as if the whole world could be ruled by logic and
reason, while every kind of tradition is seen as an anachronistic prejudice.
If one were to peruse the literature of, say, Rome at the time of the
Antonines, or Europe at the end of the 18th century, particularly France, or
that of the second half of the 19th century, these characteristics would be
easily recognised' (*S.* 2224).

Thus, the result of the cycle of demagogic plutocracy was to weaken the ruling class even more, in that every day they became less able to use force to stay in power. In order to maintain power, it was necessary to use both consent and force: 'If governments stayed in power solely by means of cunning, double-dealing and scheming, the class in which these instinct-for-combinations residues prevail would maintain its rule for a long time... But in order to govern, force is also necessary, and in so far as the instinct-for-combinations residues increase and the persistence-of-aggregations residues among the ruling class diminish, the government is less and less able to use force. An unstable equilibrium results, and revolutions are the end result' (S. 2227).

In the pre-war period, we were moving towards this state of affairs, as Pareto showed in his study of the behaviour of western European governments and of the statesmen in power at the time.[1] It was not then impossible to foresee one of the ways in which the cycle of plutocracy could be eliminated.

We have already remarked upon how much Pareto liked to compare present-day society with the Greek and Roman societies. He was struck by an analogy which he mentions again and again in all of his writings: that conditions in society today resemble those in the Roman Republic in its decline. Pareto added, still using what could be learned from other historical cycles, that it was extremely likely that the downfall of demagogic plutocracy was imminent. The history of the decline of the Roman Republic 'provides us with several attempts to overthrow legitimate regimes. In this respect, Catiline's conspiracy is somewhat analogous to the revolutionary, anarchist and other similar groups of our age. That the person in question had little to recommend him would appear to be an established fact, but it seems that he did not have any gift for the ingenious intrigues which brought wealth and power to other people, who were no more honest than he. To offset this, however, he had a courage which stopped him from giving in to oppression. He had a courageous, proud and bold disposition, was unflinching in his use of force, and stuck to the path which lay before him. A great many other people found themselves in situations similar to his, owing to the predominance of *S* in the ruling class... There were those who had been defeated by the *S* politicians, and who badly wanted a fight in which force would prevail over cunning... Catiline's conspiracy was only one of several attempts at revolt which preceded the final cataclysm, one incident among the civil wars which marked the end of the Republic and which formed in part a struggle between those who embodied first class residues and those who embodied second class residues. The latter prevailed under Augustus. With the military being given a definite role, society entered a period of stability' (*P.* 197, 198, see *S.* 2573f.). Considering the analogy drawn between the decadence of the Roman Republic and the condition of modern society, Pareto believed before the war that the cycle of demagogic plutocracy could well come to a violent end, similar to that just described.

II

While he was waiting for such an event to happen, the First World War broke out. It will be interesting to consider the opinions expressed by our author about this.

He showed himself to be in a different class from many authors on this subject. Firstly, in his usual way, he acknowledged very openly any mistakes he might have made. In the epilogue to *Fatti e teorie*, he went over what he had said during the war, and established what was correct and what was false, as if it had been written by someone else. Going over what he wrote then, one is often struck by the accuracy of his opinions. This derives from his objectivity, his indifference to what we, mere mortals, would have found at the time a little too conceited, but which has borne fruit. What Pareto said at the time would today seem obvious, but then it amounted to the heresy of 'defeatism'. Reading certain pages of the manuscript left by the Master, one gets the impression that he was not beyond feeling a certain amount of sympathy for the 'defeatists' in the various belligerent countries, since there were by then a number of sceptics, whose voices were drowned by a flood of patriotic sanctimoniousness.

At the beginning of the war, Pareto considered the causes of the conflict (*Fatti e teorie* 31f.). He referred us to a passage by Polybius, in order to demonstrate the importance of exploring deeper causes, and to show that Byzantine discussions on recent events held no scientific interest. Throughout the course of history, there had always been conflict between nations in their avid desire to expand their sphere of influence. This was true for Germany, Russia and England. Indirectly, one could also see that the conflict was between 'democratic' (that is, plutocratic) nations and 'militaristic' ones. Pareto explained why Russia was an exception, and concluded by saying: 'The arguments of the die-hard socialists concerning the European war have some validity in that the plutocrats of various countries are arguing amongst themselves, in the manner of the Roman *mercatores* and the Punic merchants' (*F.* 44).

The violation of Belgian neutrality did not surprise him. How could he have found it anything other than normal, when already in 1901 he had written (in *Vita internazionale*, 'Riposta a l'inchiesta'): 'In the unhappy event of a European war, the treaties by which Belgium and Switzerland are to remain neutral will not be respected. Each participant will behave as it pleases, that is, according to the strength of its military power.' This is exactly what happened.

Pareto, who did not give any credence to the absurd derivations of the belligerents (*F.* 377f.), tried to solve a number of problems objectively. In the *Giornale d'Italia*, for 25 September 1914 (*T.* 81n.), he wrote the following: 'It is probable that the present war will be a long one... We shall see that those who maintain that the war cannot last long, because of the difficulties with finance or supplies which certain belligerents are likely to experience, are making a serious mistake.' Were there many other economists who uttered a similar opinion after six weeks of hostilities?

Pareto was less emphatic regarding the outcome of the war. Certain pages of the *Sociologie*, concerning Athens at the time of Philip and France before 1870 and during 1913, could be interpreted as a prophecy of a German victory. In the article in which he specifically addressed this question, however, (*Scientia*, March 1915, *F.* 55), he did not arrive at any conclusion. His major impression was that it was difficult to see how either side could gain a conclusive victory. Nor did he have much sympathy for those who hoped for an idyllic peace after 'the war to end all wars'. 'When has Europe ever enjoyed a peace for so long that it seemed as if it would last forever? Since when has it been wrong for victors to invest in armaments and armies in order to maintain their hold on power, or for the vanquished to do likewise to get their revenge, or for neutral countries to adopt similar measures to maintain their independence? The fact is that those who dream of a future markedly different from the past are deliberately closing their eyes to the evidence, and entering the obscure realms of fantasy.' These ideas, which are commonplace now, offended popular opinion at the time.

As long as the war lasted, argued Pareto, people would imagine that all problems would automatically disappear when it ended. Arguing against this universally held belief, he emphasised that post-war problems would have to be faced. 'The ease of levying taxes, of issuing paper money, of borrowing immense sums of money has led governments to spend prodigally, to dissipate their countries' resources [out of which point, incidentally, came a very interesting economic discussion], and paved the way for a difficult situation in the future... Will they be able, when peace comes, to keep the large promises which they now find themselves obliged to make?... The only important matter at the moment is to overcome the enemy, that is the recipe for perfect happiness. But this path leads to serious difficulties once disillusionment sets in and it becomes clear that the problem of economic production is separate from that of the political supremacy of certain countries over others.' (*Coenobium*, July 1918. 'After Four Years of War'; *F.* 163, 167).

Therefore, governmental statements to the public have been consistently inaccurate. Pareto, on the other hand, foresaw – and with what accuracy! – two economic phenomena which occurred just as he had predicted. The first one was the depreciation of currency. In February 1916 he asked: who will pay for the inevitable reduction of the public debt? His reply was: 'The savers who have invested their savings in fixed income shares payable in currency that has lost its value. This is what has happened in the past, and this is what will doubtless continue to happen for a long time.' (*F.* 61); he often returned to this idea in other articles, but it is not worth quoting from them here (*F.* 170, 192, 212ff., 275).

There were indeed post-war economic problems, and in particular the crisis which was to come in 1920. In 1917, (*F.* 103) he believed that in general there would be an economic downturn after the war. In 1918, he expressed the following opinion (*F.* 157): 'In general, after major wars, peace is followed by a short period of economic prosperity, high prices and then a fairly or very long period of economic depression and low prices. Of course these facts, although very well known, are entirely ignored or concealed by those who want to persuade the general public that a period of unlimited prosperity will follow the present war, and in fact will be a result of it.' Immediately after the war, he continued to maintain this point of view, and tried to convince his contemporaries that an economic crisis was imminent (*F.* 268, *Resto del carlino* 16 August 1920, etc.).

On all these questions, Pareto the economist seems to have had a reasonably clear understanding of the facts.

We will now examine some of his views as a sociologist on the post-war period. In particular, we will consider his critique of national self-determination in *Rivista d'Italia*, Soc.? in July 1918 (*F.* 171, et s). It is important to note the subtlety with which Pareto, while apparently only talking about ancient history, also manages to slip in criticism: 'When Flaminius made the announcement at the Isthmian Games that Rome had decreed that all Greek cities would be free, the Greeks were rapturous with joy' [then follows this delightful quotation from Livy]: 'Esse aliquam in terris gentem quae sua impensa suo labore ac periculo bellagerat pro libertate aliorum... maria trajiciat, ne quod toto orbe terrarum injustum imperium sit, et ubique jus, fas, lex potentissima sint. [Were not precisely these derivations recited to us at the time?]'

In fact, this principle of national self-determination was simply a derivation, useful for attaining certain objective goals, but of no intrinsic value. Events proved Pareto right, since this great principle was no more respected in 1919 than it had been in 1914. Taking a lesson from history, Pareto had no confidence in the League of Nations. During the war (*F.* 147), he said that either it would have no effect whatsoever, or it would lead to dominance by one of the members of the League, and the subjugation of the others. 'It is possible that the future will be different from the past, but I would very much like to know why and how this will come about.'[2] However, an objective analysis of the League of Nations and its structure reveals that *perhaps* it contained certain aspects likely to make it an effective influence for peace,[3] contrary to our author's fixed opinions.

Once the war had ended, Pareto went on to analyse the causes of Germany's defeat. He saw in this an opportunity to apply his theory about the distribution of first and second class residues throughout the various social strata (*F.* 341ff). The German leadership had been blinded by its belief in a German destiny. Such reverence deprived them of any sense of the realities of diplomacy, and despite their victories, they saw themselves as being under incessant attack from new adversaries. 'Among the general population – the ruled, not the rulers – of the opposing countries, there was little difference from one country to another in terms of the strength of second class residues. The belief in 'German destiny', in its military might, its 'organising ability', and the doctrine of its 'vital interests' all combined to distort the judgement of the German leadership. Conversely, there was a predominance of first class residues among the leaders of the Entente, except in Russia. Therefore, in both Russia and Germany the leaders were defeated and overthrown.

The post-war political and economic measures taken by the different governments provided Pareto with another opportunity to express harsh criticisms. The first version of the Versailles Treaty was unworkable (*Secolo*, 21 February 1923), and the Allies' stance on the question of reparations was absurd: 'To discuss what a defeated Germany *must* pay is a fine exercise in legal – or rather, in pseudo-legal – sophistry on questions of international morality, equity and many other fanciful ideas. Knowing how to demand war indemnity from Germany without using the phrase, which would cause Wilson much pain, is a fine use of derivations. From a practical point of view, however, none of this replaces the necessity of finding out what Germany *can* pay, and what it is *to the victor's advantage* to demand' (*T.* 24). The armistice was followed by a period of economic and financial chaos. Pareto's assessment of the situation differed radically from the majority of contemporary views. There was general despair in the face of currency depreciation, the increased cost of living, etc.; people tried to confront these problems head on. Pareto, correctly in our view, believed this method to be absurd. A more realistic approach and a clearer grasp of the overall economic picture would reveal the futility of these endeavours.

He said: 'It is an excellent thing to take action against economic disorder but it is of little use if the root cause of the problem is not eliminated. The problem, contrary to popular belief, is not the issuing of paper money. This policy is only a sign of the wasteful policies which are being carried out, for the moment at least, without the people's knowledge. The heart of the matter is wastefulness, not only by the government but also by the nation as a whole, which wants to do less work but consume more, which is impossible. (*Resto del carlino*, 2 November 1922)... Certainly the devaluation of currency and unemployment are real ills, but it is far from certain that direct remedies are of any great use... Those who believe in the far-reaching effectiveness of these measures, those who want to combat monetary devaluation by means of foreign loans, embargoes on imports and similar ploys, and who want to combat unemployment by subsidising workers or their employers, the right to a certain amount of money, pretty useless public works, are all behaving like someone who in order to stay cool in summer and to keep warm in winter adjusts the thermometer... Moreover, unemployment and monetary devaluation do not indicate economic conditions, they can also restore the equilibrium. Everything which restricts this influence, in effect prevents the restoration of the equilibrium (*Resto*, 26 October 1921)... The basic problems in Europe are not the fall of the mark, the krone, or other currencies, but the economic, political and social conditions which have given rise to this depreciation. Let us not be under any illusion: as long as the cause remains, the effects will follow. Only by working on the cause can one bring about a change in the effects. Everything else is an illusion, even a falsity. (*Secolo*, 16 September 1922).

The deep-seated decadence of the bourgeoisie following the war (*Is.*) perhaps explains this inability to grasp reality. In the light of sociological analysis, it seems that the bourgeoisie, along with the rest of society, was experiencing a profound crisis. One of the most remarkable manifestations of this phenomenon was the disintegration of central power. Pareto studied this crisis in *Trasformazione della democrazia*, and he made some very important historical and psychological observations concerning the lessening of governmental authority (*T.* 29 et s.). Sociology is not sufficiently developed for Pareto's studies of this period to be seen as definitive. This small book is nevertheless very unusual and always interesting.

III

It is possible to consider Fascism in Italy as a temporary and isolated phenomenon, but it could also be seen as the start of a fundamental change to the cycle of plutocracy.

Pareto, to the author

Could not all these factors signify the decline of demagogic plutocracy? We will remember that it was under threat from those who wanted to combat machinations with might, and would not be afraid of using violence to gain power. Pareto returns to his favourite example by quoting from Sallust and concluding thus: 'This speech by Catiline could well have been uttered by the Bolsheviks of our own times and expresses attitudes which have been, are being, and will be perceived amongst resolute people who are not content to remain the compliant victims of the subtle ploys of those who do not use force. Catiline and his co-fighters fell as heroes at Fiesole. But the sentiments inspiring them remained. Caesar, then Augustus, profited from a similar frame of mind and were victorious as a result' (*F.* 244, 245). In the same way, says Pareto, Bolshevism, the Spartacists, etc., can be defeated and even destroyed, but the beliefs which they embody will remain in a different guise.

In fact, these sentiments were not strong enough for Communism to prevail in western Europe. Considering the success of Fascism where Communism had failed (*Gerarchia*, January 1923), Pareto came to the following conclusion: the Bolshevik mobs who occupied Italian factories, etc., sought only material gain. They had few if any noble ideals, and no willingness to make costly sacrifices for the realisation of their 'dream'. The 'march on Rome' was a totally different matter. Those who carried it out embodied extremely strong second class residues.

This brings us to an assessment of the relation between Pareto's thought and Fascism. On the whole, it can be said that this social phenomenon proved to be a very accurate demonstration of his theories.[4]

In certain places (*S.* 2190, 2191), Pareto describes in abstract terms the onset of a revolution which benefits a new *B* élite to the detriment of the former *A* government. There are certain passages in this description which prefigure the rise of Fascism. Let us suppose, he says, that humanitarianism is constantly gaining in strength among the ruling class, the latter becoming each day less and less capable of defending itself, of using force to maintain law and order. 'Such a country is travelling down the road to ruin.' This was more or less the situation which obtained in Italy in 1922: the central power had lost all its authority. There was a growth of *B* amongst the governed, that is of men who were given to using violence. 'By using force without restraint, not only do the *B* reduce the *A* to poverty, but they also kill some of them, and, to tell the truth, in so doing they perform a task which is of as much use as destroying vermin [!]. The *B* bring a great number of group enthusiasms [second class residues] into the government of society... Consequently, society gains stability and strength. The country is saved from ruin and experiences a renaissance'. This description can quite obviously be applied to Italy in the postwar period.

Moreover, the origins of most of Italy's present rulers, and particularly of their leader, are well known. Pareto wrote of the revolutionary uprisings in Romagna in June 1914 (*S.* 2480): 'We are witnessing nothing less than the struggle between the fox and the lion. One side believes it can win by trickery alone, and totally dismisses any suggestion of virility or courage. Its opponents, on the other hand, *in the manner of the men of Avanti, are virile and loyal, and it is this virility and loyalty that, sooner or later, will make their victory a certainty, which, in the final analysis, will be useful to the whole country.* The fox, using his shrewd tricks, will remain safe for quite a while, but the day will perhaps come when the lion will bring down the fox with a well-aimed blow from his claws, and the struggle will be ended.' Pareto then contrasted the extremists' attitude with that of the reformist socialists, who used humanitarian derivations – evidence of their weakness of character. And indeed, they were the ones currently being devoured by the lion.

All this leads us to ask the following question: was Pareto a 'Fascist'? The question is not relevant when our author's scientific writings are under consideration. But since being a Fascist is seen by some to be a matter of great pride, while to others it is an abomination, it is as well to ask whether Pareto deserved such extremes of acclaim and opprobrium. In spite of the imprecision of this phrase 'to be a Fascist',[5] it is easy to give an answer by quoting from the following passage in the magazine *Gerarchia* (May 1923, editor: B. Mussolini) in which M. Volt, in a study on Pareto's works wrote: 'From a subjective point of view, Pareto is not an apostle of Fascism, but he has been its prophet.' This quite plausible opinion is supported by the most convincing public and private testimony.[6] In fact, Pareto never formed a clearly defined political point of view. He was singularly opposed to modern parliamentary government. There was only one occasion on which he expressed an opinion on this question, which was in a letter addressed to Cremone's *Idea* in January 1898. He declared himself to be a 'federal republican'.[7]

Whatever he was, Pareto not only refused to become an admirer of the new regime, but also spoke about it with great circumspection. Before Fascism became an actual political movement, he refused to comment on it because, to him, the factual analysis did not appear to be conclusive. 'Undoubtedly,' he says (*Giornale d'Italia* 24 September 1922), 'it is not possible to assert that changes similar to those which brought the Roman Republic down are not on the agenda, but (*Secolo* 17 August 1922) a dictatorship needs a dictator, whether it be a Caesar, an Augustus, a Robespierre, a Napoleon I or III, a Lenin or any of the other figures of which history provides countless examples. At the moment, such a man has not arisen in Italy.' Pareto made no attempt in the articles he wrote before the establishment of Fascism to give any praise to that creed.[8]

Fascism's moment of glory had come. Pareto recorded the fact, but he did not enthuse over it. I questioned him about this. He answered (31 October 1922): 'Read the first article in *Temps* of 29 October entitled "The Fascist Tendency". Although it seems to give a clear and objective idea of Fascism, this impression is partly false. I do not believe that any newspaper will correct the errors in this analysis by the *Temps*. It will either be confirmed or contradicted by other derivations. However, history remains and gives us an infinite number of examples of the contrast between idealised goals and actual achievements. When the Roman Empire became Christian, perhaps it aimed for the same ideals as those in the Gospels. But it was very far from realising them in practice.'

Pareto always had a strong streak of independence. We will consider another example of this. Some readers of his observations on plutocratic governments might think he was a supreme reactionary. And yet, in 1898, he came to the assistance of the Italian socialists. Later on, he accused the persecutors of Catholics in France.[9] Now that his country finally had a dynamic government, Pareto, without actually siding with the opposition, immediately took up the cause of liberty. Certain people have called his last-ever article 'Pareto's political testament' (*Giornale economico*, September 1923). He called for freedom of the press in Italy, and exhorted the government to be moderate.[10] But his ideas were perhaps even more clearly expressed in the official Fascist organ of the government which had just recognised that he was worthy of public honours. Thus, in *Gerarchia* (July 1923, 'Libertà'), Pareto expresses the following view: 'Fascism is not only good because it is dictatorial – as with any other system of government it can be perverted by a corrupted dictator – but because so far its achievements have been good.'[11] Additionally Pareto mentioned several pitfalls to be avoided, namely: (1) bellicose exploits; (2) suppression of free speech: 'It is necessary to have a largely free press'; (3) excessive taxation: neither the rich nor the poor should be under a crushing burden of taxation; (4) association with religion: Fascism should not throw itself into the arms of the Church; (5) academic freedom: '*teaching at university levels should not be subject to any restrictions. People should be free to teach Newton's theories as well as Einstein's, Marx's theories as well as those of the historical school.*' This is what the reactionary die-hard, the critic of the socialist systems, the master of the 'mathematical school' wrote a few weeks before his death. May his critics emulate this admirable example of scientific impartiality, this great example of tolerance.

Nobody can today predict the future of Fascism. Perhaps it will not survive some miscalculation in economic or foreign policy, or the death of its leaders. Again, it is possible that Fascism will endure for many years to come, and that similar movements will emerge elsewhere. Whatever happens, at the moment this social movement appears to have vindicated Pareto's argument, and it should be recognised that his attitude towards it was that of an upright man.

IV

Thus the cycle running through society can be broken by violent movements, which seize power from the demagogic plutocracy. According to Pareto, however, there is another threat to society, which he called its 'growing crystallisation'.[12] Given the form of his writings, he never clarified the relation between these two phenomena. It seems to me that he considered them to be independent of each other, since when he looked at the facts he saw the two possibilities.

In certain respects, as we have seen, society exists in a state of equilibrium which is permanently unstable. However, seen from an economic rather than political viewpoint, society is moving towards a state of greater stability.[13] Looking at the history of societies over a long time, it becomes apparent that there is an alternation between periods of individualism and periods of state control of industry and public services and other types of government control. There are periods in which economic activity has few constraints, and there are others in which it is hindered by an ever-expanding network.

'Experience shows us that these oscillations can be of variable import-ance and duration; but it does not point to any civilised people amongst whom no such undulations can be observed. It is therefore not very likely, at least for the moment, that there could be any society that is totally with-out them (*S*. 2553). Pareto studied (*S*. 2607ff.) this cycle in Roman history. He showed that the 'crystallisation' of society in the Byzantine Empire had followed a period of liberty as a natural progression. It had not been imposed from above; rather, the citizens had wanted it. 'This phenomenon can be more fully understood by observing contemporary events which are largely similar. Our national prosperity is – albeit in part – the result of the freedom in social and economic terms, that existed during part of the nine-teenth century. But now the crystallisation has begun as it did in the Roman Empire. The people want it, and it often seems to increase prosperity' (*S*. 2553). The liberalism of 1860 increasingly gave way to protectionism, state socialism, government control, etc.

'In conclusion, it is clear that we are travelling along a curve similar to that which Roman society followed after the Empire was founded, and which, after ushering in a period of prosperity, lasted until the coming of decadence' (ibid.). This seems to be the path that all societies are follow-ing. However, it is difficult to make definite predictions about this subject. We do not have a crystal ball: 'History never repeats itself, and it is extremely unlikely, unless one believes in the "yellow peril", that the next period of prosperity will result from another barbarian invasion. It would be even less likely that prosperity would follow an internal revolution, which would put power into the hands of people who have an abundance of second class residues, who know how to use force and are able and willing to do so. But these distant possibilities belong more to the realm of fantasy than to the study of experimental science.'

Pareto's theories on the future state of society were curious and interest-ing, but – and this is a point I wish to stress – they were not part of any 'social system' posited by him, unlike, for example, Marx's theories. What makes them so interesting is the fact that he tried to interweave economic, political and social history, and in so doing made deductive observations. Since his conclusions were, at least in part, contrary to his own sentiments (as was the growing state control of society), it is very likely that they were solely the result of objective enquiry, and not, as with Marx, an expression of his own hopes. Pareto also had the great advantage over Marx, as he did over Spencer, that he did not assign to society a limiting state, an asymptote of the curve that it was following. Therefore, his deductive reasoning was strictly scientific, in contrast to digressions about the golden age, industrial society, the static state, earthly paradise, the socialist state of the future, etc., concepts which embody a finite perception of the way societies are organised, whether it be in their origin or their completion. Pareto's analysis is not necessarily complete and correct. Is it correct? Only time will tell, in a future which will doubtless not be known by either the writer or the reader of these words. So there is no point in discussing the matter! Is it complete? No one would be able to argue that it is. For instance, two very important phenomena are totally omitted. Firstly, the relative economic decline of contemporary Europe, which the theorist of social undulations does not even mention. Secondly, there is the question of feminism, which the theorist of élites and their movements ought not to have forgotten. These examples could be multiplied.

However, what we find most remarkable in our study of Pareto's social theories is the high-mindedness of his thought, also his absolute candour, and that rare gift of being self-critical. By recognising his errors, and qualifying his own theories with question marks, he confirmed his wisdom.

7 Fascism and the Impartial Theoretician

Alfonso de Pietri-Tonelli

We must now look, by way of comparison, at two aspects of Pareto's activity which are by nature in contrast and tend to be consecutive in time. We must look at Pareto the practical and theoretical politician, and compare him to Pareto the impartial theoretician and scientist.

When we describe Pareto as a politician we mean the Pareto who was involved in politics, who took part in political struggles in general and influenced economic policy in particular; Pareto the advocate of certain general policies and economic policy in particular and the formulator and disseminator of theories of political or economic policy aimed at influencing and changing the course of men's actions. We do not mean the Pareto whose development in politics was influenced by the major political theorists, particularly the teachings of Machiavelli's *Principe*, whose aim was to develop political theory merely for the sake of knowledge and explain concrete political happenings in the light of theories resulting from Pareto's activities as a sociologist in particular and as a scientist in general.

Pareto's different attitudes towards concrete political activity are marked by his changing from being a party man and scientist at the same time to being purely and simply a scientist. These two attitudes were each criticised for different reasons: the former by the members of opposition parties, the latter by various party supporters who considered it impossible, inhuman, to be objective and impartial even as regards one aspect of one's personal activity.

We must briefly describe the background to this change and where it led to, before considering the scientific movements which stem from Pareto. This means highlighting the vitality of Pareto's theories which, far from becoming crystallised, tend to develop in their fundamental principles and give rise to other scientific movements. Our conclusions deal with Pareto's essence, the real and potential value of Pareto's school of thought.

Pareto's activities as a politician were secondary, occasional and transitory. We can see him as a politician in some of his early writings and speeches which were contentious and occasionally violent, such as those in the *Giornale degli economisti*, in some parts of the *Cours* and in writings spread over many years in various journals and newspapers. This is also discernible when Pareto was the losing candidate in the political elections for the Pistoia area.

Reading these writings it seems that, especially as time went by, Pareto followed the political activities he criticised more with the eye of the scholar than the passion of a party man. This was the reason he often wrote very penetrating things for different types of readers in articles and brief notes which would be difficult to retrace even for those who were able to follow them. This type of minor activity is not to be considered a worthless popularisation inasmuch as it served increasingly to test the applicability of his theories. The lectures at the University of Lausanne and the brief courses that he held in Paris and Bologna also served to clarify his ideas. His voluminous correspondence with both the most famous thinkers and young students from all over the world served the same purpose. His conversations with varied and increasingly numerous visitors to Switzerland (who were, whoever they were, always well received, or given hospitality at Villa Angora) served also to keep him in touch with current ideas.

Pareto's first political writings show evidence of his preparation in the classics of economics and the influence of Ferrara. The opportunity and the stimulus which the struggles taking place at that time gave him, to write about economics and economic policy are evident here. He was always fundamentally in favour of a *laissez faire* economic policy and liberalism in politics. He described himself openly, in fact, as belonging to the old Liberal Party. He was against interventionism although he recognised at the same time the social usefulness of the two opposite tendencies, which, by curbing each other brought about advantageous solutions. He was against monopolies, against protectionism and in favour of free trade. For a long time he was happy to have been able to demonstrate by rigorous analysis that monopolies and protectionism give rise to transfers of goods which are always accompanied by the destruction of wealth. He was happy to correct an error of Cournot on the effect of customs duty.

This is Pareto's attitude in the *Cours* and its related writings. His attitude in the *Manuale* is quite different. Here Pareto accuses the author of the *Cours* and other writings of having maintained that peace and economic and political freedom are the best means to ensure the good of the people, without giving any proof of this. Similar implicit statements did not derive from the facts, as they should have done in a book dedicated to the study of facts, but originated for the most part in the feelings of the author.

In the *Systèmes*, among his criticisms of many other utopias, we find Pareto's criticism of the liberal utopia and the reasons for its decline. In the

Manuale he finds an error of synthesis in the author of the *Cours* who declares himself against protectionism. The fact that protection usually destroys wealth is not enough to condemn it. When the economic consequences of a measure have been demonstrated, one element for the overall judgement on the appropriateness of adopting the measure exists, but it will not be the only element to be taken into account. Despite much condemnation, people have pursued protectionism and have not been ruined by it when they were prosperous nor did protectionism help them to make good, it must be added, when they found themselves, as at present, in a depression. In the *Systèmes* and especially in the *Manuale* he considers the social aspect of protectionism and shows that, in an expansionary period, it is capable of creating, through the destruction of wealth or even by hindering its creation, much greater quantities of wealth by transferring those goods saved by *rentiers* to speculators who destroy them but are also capable of multiplying them.

In the logical argument typical of theoretical economics, the role of the abstract hypothesis of perfect competition remains unchanged, in domestic and international trade, in production, etc., and the theoretical consequences of this type of behaviour are sometimes close to reality but more often are quite far from it. If we consider a theoretical hypothesis derived from some but not all of reality, it does not mean we accept that the hypothesis is altogether and always real or feasible; much less does it mean we take it upon ourselves to act on such a hypothesis because it is socially useful or good for certain purposes.

Similar confusion exists only amongst those who are not conversant with the scientific study of the economy or those who wish to spread their hasty, unrealistic theories, to avoid the toil of learning the old laborious theories based on reality.

The darts Pareto had flung at the protectionists were not withheld when it came to those guilty of malpractice in money and banking, of misappropriation by government and banks. His style had become more bitter and violent. Writing about those who wanted to have their evil political arts justified by pseudo-scientific cavils, he said that no mathematics existed with which to cover up the shameful actions of governments, which took advantage of the power the law gave them over the banks of issue to extort money for their friends and followers and even for festivities by which to corrupt the electorate.

Pareto's judgement of politics, like that of Sorel, was inflexibly moral. This can be seen beneath the veneer of bitter sarcasm and the appearance of scientific coldness. Like Sorel, Pareto kept his eye and mind on the present especially when linking it to the past in order to offend his contemporaries less; Pareto, however, was not really like Sorel who was much more partial and passionate and talked of historical personalities or groups in order to attack those of the present to which he had a profound aversion. Pareto was aristocratic by nature, inasmuch as he had faith in the few that he saw rising over the many in all epochs and maybe in those who dominate their fellow men. In democratic times, Pareto rose above the dominant faction and did not allow himself to be taken in by democratic illusions, in fact he demonstrated the plutocratic trajectory of democracy, condemned its waste and derided its deceptions.

By instinct he was a conservative, he was not attracted by socialism which appealed to so many, nor by its humanitarian variety which attracted many fugitives from the decadent ruling class, particularly its many incoherent members. He did, however, defend political freedoms, even in favour of socialists, and humanely assisted political refugees, thrown out of Italy during the period of reaction against the first socialist movements.

He was sceptical by nature, maybe also on account of the political environment in which he lived and the scientific one in which he developed. He knew and had studied all types of religion from every epoch and recognised their functions and social value too well to not emphasise the often repeated error in history of believing that men can manage without some form of religion or repress their feelings for long. He hated the simulated forms of religion in which he saw no social usefulness; to him they were a sign of weakness and decadence in a society. He was strongly opposed to them. He was also opposed to teetotallers, vegetarians and the disciples of what he regarded as hypocritical virtues; it was as though he wished to express himself in favour of a healthy pagan joy in food and drink and other healthy instincts which help to perpetuate strong and vigorous races.

Although he was knowledgeable about history and saw the virtues and vices of different peoples he was never infatuated with any one people in particular. He said that it was the great men of one's own country, if any, that should be imitated, so as to be oneself in the best possible way. He was referring to his own country in particular, since he felt himself, not without pride, to be Italian, but he also felt himself to be a citizen of a much vaster nation, the ideal nation of science which does not make one forget the real, smaller (even if it is great) nation although the real, smaller one makes one forget the vaster one. 'Because I spoke the truth about politicians who were destroying Italy, I was accused of speaking ill of Italy', he wrote indignantly, when this was used as a pretext to deny him, who had held high the name of Italy, an honour which would have honoured equally both giver and receiver.

'This poverty does not affect me' he added, adding bitter scorn to his invective.

A colleague from an American university who was familiar with both Pareto's writings and the Italian language, asked me if the *Trattato di sociologia generale* that was being translated in America could really be described as the bible of Fascism or the *Capital* of the new social religion which originated and was established by the use of force in Italy and is in the process of spreading to other countries. I replied calmly, without reflecting much, though I understood the doubts of my colleague, that this description would not have displeased Pareto and maybe he would have been gratified if it helped to get his theories known in a country which was still so caught up by democratic false modesty. He cared, and rightly so, about the diffusion of his works.

We must point out that, doubtless, if Pareto had a political party it was above all his own party. A Pareto who is tied to a party of the type in democratic countries, with their internal and external strife, is unthinkable. Acceptance of a party of belonging, as the Italian Fascist party could be defined, is rather more comprehensible. However the portrait of Pareto during the war as a venerable but cold old man without passions or sympathy for his fellow men whose minds and institutions were in turmoil, an unmoved and unmovable observer at Céligny, isolated from events and intent on observing them coldly from a distance, as an astronomer observes the movements of celestial bodies, a Pareto intent on cataloguing the facts of war and judging them with indifference if not arrogance and scorn, is a caricature. This part of Pareto, which could perhaps be criticised, is not, nor can it be all of Pareto; even if the protest which he is said to have made about this during the war on the occasion of his jubilee celebrations is nowhere to be found in the press reports.

Pareto did not let himself be influenced by sympathies or rather by undying aversions as Sorel did. The latter, who supported certain political groups, usually in a transitory fashion, was thought to do this in order to annoy some people or to influence others. Pareto's least hint of agreement has great value if we consider it comes from someone with such an independent, unprejudiced and realistic character. He was a man who was used to being led by reason and reflection and little inclined to being led astray by sentiment, or being influenced by the superficial appearance of things. Because he lived outside his own country, he had already reached a point in his spiritual life where even the closest things are seen from a distance.

There is, it seems, clear evidence also in his writings that Pareto acted as an instigator of the decisive actions of Fascism. In what was called Pareto's political testimony, we find judgements and advice on government by force and government by consensus, on apparent majority government and real minority government, on elected and chosen bodies, on words and facts, on real feelings and simulated feelings.

It can certainly be said that the political and economic movement which best corresponded to Pareto's inclinations was the liberal *laissez faire* one in which he participated; but it may also be said, that the political movement in which he could participate spiritually and which corresponded to his inclinations in his later years was the Fascism of violent conquest, that of the early Fascists who had been raised in an environment which had developed in them the necessary qualities to ensure victory.

It must be objectively observed, however, that both Pareto and Sorel were curious to observe at close quarters the new social experiments, especially those which proved to be vigorous and daring. Pareto considered Fascism's political aspects – that is, the use of force, discipline and authority – but not the political, economic and social aspects of corporatism which developed after his death.

Pareto, who had tried to base his theories on reality, trying to make social reality understandable to some degree, was a scholar rather than a teacher, dictator or reformer. He was therefore not surprised by the extraordinary events of 1914 and thus had no cause to marvel at them. Moreover he had no need to recognise errors of judgement, to renege either the whole or a part of his teachings, to abandon his intellectual heritage like cast-off clothing, as so many others had done who had allowed themselves to cherish unpardonable illusions or tried to make others indulge in dangerous dreams.

As we have said, Pareto was looking for a means of testing the theories of the *Trattato* experimentally. He did not live to see the consolidation of Fascism after its triumph. If he had done so he would have seen many members of the plutocracy, such as the 'sharks' who had been the object of his sarcasm, ruined. He would have seen the liquidation and the rebirth of a large part of the private economy weighing on the overburdened finances of the state. He would have had something to say about the financial hospitals created for sick, incurable, chronically ill or convalescent firms. He would have seen the beginnings of corporative Fascism. He would have seen those general aspects of Fascism which are common to different countries spreading, and the increasing importance of political and associational ties in the economy. In addition to corporatism and Bolshevism, he would have been interested in Hitlerism and Rooseveltism, etc. He would have followed the continual changes in social life, the perennial succession in the history of movements whose particular forms are new though their substance is less so, and whose general forms tend to be repetitive.

Pareto did not finish the critical work he had vowed to write, nor would he ever have been able to finish it, since he would have always found new subjects for study in the flux of social life. His long days were always full. He died while the world was in great turmoil: only vague directions in the tangle of movements were and are visible, so that strong doubts exist as to whether certain tendencies are to be connected to transitory circumstances, peculiar to a certain period. These might last for a limited time or might be of much longer duration and therefore leave their mark on human history, characterising it for several generations.

It would be a vain and puerile rhetorical exercise to ask ourselves what Pareto would have thought about the various things which currently agitate our minds and torment our souls and then answer in one way or another. As it would be useless, on the other hand, to try to remake history, with hindsight, to say how certain actions should have been undertaken or considered by certain groups at any given time. It is important, however, to establish how those actions were accomplished and considered, because this is the only way to realise the significance and understand the actions and behaviour of the members of those groups.

The problem with assessing the relationship between Pareto's thought and Fascism is to know how corporatism takes account, where possible, of the political wisdom which Pareto accumulated in the study of human society and set out in the theories of the *Trattato*.

Sociological theory has as its immediate, direct aim the explanation of action, and only indirectly that of guiding it. However, it can be assumed, as perhaps Pareto himself might have done, that Fascism has already experimented the test of social reality in real life during the difficult period of social and economic depression, without needing to ask for hypothetical tests from the dead however great they were, as indeed Pareto was.

* * *

Although it would be desirable to have a certain criterion by which to classify thinkers synthetically on the basis of their general prestige as scientists, whatever their field of investigation or the judgement they have received therein, no such criterion exists. Nor do criteria exist on which they can be classified according to what they have contributed to the world of thought in general, to the common patrimony of all thinkers in all sciences as distinct from what is particular to an individual science.

If we were to look for an appropriate criterion by which to judge thinkers, it could only be their vocation, their aptitude, and their training to deal with scientific and factual questions, the ways in which they deal with reality, and how they formulate problems. They should be judged by their views, their methods of investigation and their results; by what is common to all the different sciences in the above.

Turning my attention to a public not only of social scientists, but also of scientists of the more advanced sciences, to which the social sciences are so indebted, I would like to emphasise Pareto's value as a scientist in general terms, his attitude, methods and results, in short that which serves to qualify a scientist whatever his science.

Pareto was essentially a scientist and in this lay his greatness. We might also say Pareto was a scientist *tout court*.

This is manifest in all his writings, even those unconnected with science, and the scientific approach is gradually emphasised as his writings proceed until it becomes the predominant, almost the exclusive one. It can be inferred not only from the principles that Pareto, like many others, affirms, but above all from the way he applies them and his results.

We wish to make a generic scientific appraisal of the theories, their application and the results which Pareto obtained in the field of social research. 'The principal aim of my studies,' he wrote in 1917, in what was to be his last speech in public (to thank the guests at the festivities for his jubilee), 'has always been to apply experimental methods to the social sciences of which economics is but a part, methods which have given such brilliant results in the natural sciences.' He had expressed himself not very differently twenty years previously in the preface to the *Cours*.

Consequently we must start from hypotheses which are as close as possible to reality and use the logical tools of the most perfect paradigms. It is well known that mathematics provides the tool used by the physical sciences. Theories must be tested by observation, inasmuch as theory deals with an imaginary and simplified reality, which does not coincide with concrete and complex reality but forms a part of it. Thus rational economics ideally separates a certain category of actions, the economic ones, from the reality of human action, or, what amounts to the same thing, it considers an abstract man who only performs economic actions. Such abstractions are the basis of every science, and only those who are devoid of any notion of science can interpret them equivocally. With the help of mathematics, rational economics takes into account the most complex relations and, contrary to popular opinion, provides, by definition, the abstraction which is closest to reality and the nearest approximation to the way economic changes take place. Sociology goes one step further, taking into consideration a much wider field of human action. There are, however, limits to the application of quantitative methods in sociology, due to the rather more undeveloped stage of the discipline and maybe also because the types of calculus most suited to it are still unknown. Its theories, however, which deal with a wider range of social reality, could be subjected to less imperfect tests.

Pareto's methodology of the social sciences shows the importance of logical tools in scientific thought. The least imperfect forms of these are quantitive and mathematical and demonstrate the close link between the development of those sciences which apply quantitative methods and mathematics, the supplier of these quantitative tools. Thus, in general, do the various sciences influence each other. The progress of mathematics hence allows those sciences which apply mathematics to advance; by supplying the most suitable tools for investigation, it opens up new possibilities and wider horizons. Progress in the sciences which apply mathematics creates new methodological requirements and thus stimulates the development of particular branches of mathematics and mathematics in general. Knowledge is furthered by the fertile exchange between mathematicians and the scientists who apply mathematics. Sometimes mathematicians are the pathbreakers, while the scientists who apply mathematics follow their lead. At other times the same people push both branches of knowledge forward simultaneously: mathematicians who both provide the tool and apply it, and those scientists who, stimulated by the needs of their discipline, cause mathematics to forge ahead by perfecting the implements of their investigation. I do not need to furnish examples, which you all know well, in both the history of mathematics and the history of science, two kinds of history of which it may be said that the former is the basis of the latter but the latter tends to blend with the former in as much as scientific thought is mathematical.

I remember having heard Professor Einstein, who formulated the theory of relativity, paying homage in a speech at the University of Padua, to Professor Ricci Curbastro, for having established the fundamental outline of absolute differential calculus many years ago, thus providing the necessary logical mathematical tool for the formulation of the theory of relativity.

It is well known that hereditary[1] mechanics only became possible when the concept of function was extended. This was achieved by transporting the theories relative to the passage from the finite to the infinitesimal, and from the discontinuous to the continuous (infinitesimal calculus) into the field of the theory of functions with the preparation of functional calculus.

The whole of infinitesimal calculus can be thought of as the first chapter of this. Hereditary mechanics demonstrates the phenomena, in which hysteresis is important, with greater precision and this applies to hereditary biology and, as we shall see, to hereditary economics also. If the application of the more advanced methods of the physical sciences is used as a criterion, two classes of sciences can be distinguished in general, just as we have already seen two groups of schools of economic thought. We place the sciences which are tied to the less imperfect logical methods in the first class. The disciplines which do not employ the logical mathematical methods belong in the second class. Those sciences using logical mathematical methods are more advanced and can make more progress; they are to be found at the highest levels of scientific thought and can take advantage of relevant improvements in logical mathematical method which can be compared to the mechanics of scientific thought.

It is well known that mathematical analysis only supplies the quantitative tool and the less imperfect method: it is not free from its own limitations. In fact this quantitative tool is not sufficient by itself; it functions on the basis of certain assumptions that imply definitions. These assumptions must be adequate, that is, simple enough for an agile use of mathematics, complex enough to reflect reality. If the assumptions do not correspond to reality or are incorrect, mathematics does not have the force to give a basis to unsound reasoning nor to correct it if it is faulty. The application of mathematics can, however, lead to improved assumptions and, if necessary, their substitution after the results obtained by calculus are compared with reality through observation or experimentation. Moreover, mathematical analysis enables procedures which have brought about progress in other sciences or other sectors of a more advanced science to be applied to less advanced sciences or less advanced sectors of a science. Past efforts would be nullified if every science had to start from the beginning in building up procedures which could serve several disciplines. It would, for example, be wasted energy to reconstruct the same procedures for hereditary biology or hereditary economics which serve for hereditary mechanics, given that such procedures have already been developed in a very satisfactory fashion and experimented to great advantage by research in physics.

There have been several attempts in physics, biology and the social sciences to bring the various disciplines and the various parts of the same disciplines from the pre-mathematical qualitative stage to the mathematical quantitative stage and from there to push them further ahead once this stage had been reached.

Once a discipline has reached the point at which it can use quantitative analysis, the most appropriate tools must be used in order not to postpone further development. This is not a question of taste or opportuneness but a question of development, of life. Neither intelligent verbal reasoning nor escapes into laziness can take the place of the penetrating refinements of analysis.

The objections or doubts of non-mathematicians who are barred from a large part of the world of modern science, just as once those who did not know Latin were barred from the world of knowledge, cannot prevent the use of mathematics. It has spread to an increasing number of disciplines from Galileo's times to the times of Pareto, despite opposition which can be traced to the same Peripatetics whom Galileo scorned. Non-mathematicians are not aware, usually, that they have to solve problems of quantity and they solve them badly due to the lack of appropriate methods. Besides, the fact that they deal with things they know nothing about or know about vaguely or indirectly, deprives their judgement of any value and authority. Their work could be the subject of an interesting chapter on the psychology of non-scientific investigation.

The criticisms of mathematicians regarding the application of mathematical analysis to other disciplines and sectors of these, are more valid. Such criticisms do not usually query the application in general, but the limits, the means and the particulars, as for example the question of the competence of a given type of calculus (infinitesimal calculus, calculus of probability, functional calculus, etc.) in a given field; these criticisms have a different weight, they are the most useful criticisms or rather the only criticisms which can be useful.

The second class of disciplines that we distinguished earlier consists of the descriptive, literary disciplines which are not linked to any phase in the logical mathematical approach. They are less advanced, non-scientific, and thus cannot profit from scientific progress which derives from the use of mathematics. At times they develop independently, at others they are associated with political, philosophical, religious or artistic movements and have great extra-scientific value when they set themselves useful purposes and are not just an end in themselves.

However, sometimes the second class disciplines find themselves in a phase of transition to the first class, by means of the collection of descriptive material and research that substitutes quantitative notions for qualitative ones. This research usually begins in an arithmetical and geometric form and prepares the ground for an analysis that presupposes the transition from complex real elements to more simple abstract elements, considered on the basis of appropriate assumptions. To hazard a guess about the probable scientific future of a second class discipline, it is therefore necessary to see whether it is a discipline which is in the preparatory stage of this transition to the first class or not. Pareto's writings bear witness to his constant preoccupation with questions of method and his efforts to benefit from the methods of those who built up modern science. He was a scientist, that is a mathematician by vocation and training just as all modern scientific minds are mathematical. Following the way paved by Cournot and Walras, he tried to make use of those procedures to which the most advanced physical sciences of his time, especially mechanics, owed their progress. These procedures are those of infinitesimal calculus. He applied them not only to economics but also wherever possible to sociology. It must be emphasised that Pareto was a mathematician and could be nothing else even when he did not employ symbols but used the concepts or methods of reasoning, that is of determining, posing and solving problems, which are characteristic of mathematics.

His approach starts from a scientific determinism implicit in mechanical models and initially he pushes this determinism to an act of faith as in the last paragraph of the *Cours*, ascribing an absolute value to the scientific regularity of social acts and to those natural facts which cannot be supposed to be subject to historical laws. Subsequently he modifies his determinism, following the tendencies which were dominant in scientific thought, and states that regularities are no longer an absolute necessity, but that their observation and the impression that everything behaves as though they existed, are. When the facts do not seem to present any regularities, this is due to our ignorance. This determinism is extended naturally to economics based on rational principles and to sociology, where non-logical actions are considered to be linked to residues whose distribution varies.

He considers the simultaneous interactions between several quantities rather than the actions of one quantity over another in economic and social actions. When it is possible to overcome ensuing difficulties, he expresses these relationships with systems of distinct and consistent equations, as many as the number of the unknowns to be determined. However, usually the formulation in terms of equations will not lead to the finding of arithmetical solutions, which are difficult to find unless we consider special numerical cases, but allows an undoubtedly mathematical analysis. This is worth attempting in itself as an analytical effort and can stand even after changes in principles take place. This use of equations is wrongly under-estimated because it is not realised that it is not an end in itself but allows mathematical properties to yield regularities concerning the group of actions under consideration and allows the experimental verification of these regularities to take place and therefore the re-examination of the hypotheses and the limits to their validity.

In attempting to untangle the complex web of circumstances which constitutes the flow of economic and social life, Pareto's investigations proceed in successive phases from the general to the particular or from the simple to the complex, as the use of mathematical procedures permits. In an initial synthetic phase, the fundamental characteristics are sought on the basis of an ideal simplified outline of the object. In subsequent phases, on the basis of already established properties, other characteristics are established by making successive hypotheses. This process continues, thus gradually complicating the research and approaching closer to reality. This is the goal of theory in every science. Moreover, the nearer reality the theories are (ranging from a maximum in astrology to a minimum in sociology) the less complex that reality and the more advanced the theories will be. This provides the criterion by which to judge the scientific value of the theories, since science must be kept distinct from faith. Science can be said to be that which can be proved using the most suitable means available at the time, inasmuch as even the value of an experiment is relative to people, means, times, places, etc. and is not completely certain, although preferable to other methods, since it is the least uncertain.

When Pareto says he wishes to study economics and sociology in the same way that physical sciences are studied, he wishes to show that he will not be sidetracked by *a priori* assumptions nor accept preconstructed results, and will only pursue knowledge and reality. He aims at understanding, nót trying to change reality. Thus, if we wish to understand Pareto our frame of reference must be knowledge for knowledge's sake though this may seem esoteric to some.

By keeping theoretical ends distinct from practical ends, and the construction of a theory from its practical applications, tasks which presuppose different attitudes and correspond to different needs, we can keep theory free from practical constraints. Thus theoretical research is carried out without practical concerns and practice is freed from theoretical constraints so that practical applications are carried out without theoretical hindrance. This means that one need is not subordinated to another but at the same time the existence of links that naturally tie theoretical and applied sciences, and the indirect practical ends of theoretical research even in the social sciences and the influence that theory, including economic and social theory, can have on man's behaviour are acknowledged. Knowledge of economic theories supposedly helps to avoid some, but certainly not all, mistakes in economic policy just as knowledge of political theories can supposedly contribute to the avoidance of some political mistakes and permit the perpetration of what seems to be an economic mistake for reasons of political expediency. Theory calls up reason which is not the strongest of human characteristics and usually abandons the field to stronger characteristics.

Pareto was conscious of the contingent, provisional value of theory and its relativity to time, place, people and the means of observation and experimentation. Theories are not constructed to dominate facts and action but to be dominated by them. A theory can only have the value of a hypothesis, designed to summarise a variable number of actions or facts. It behaves as though it obeyed given laws and establishes consistencies which are only more or less probable or at the most very probable; they are never definitive except in the illusions of their formulators. Theory has to be upheld as long as it is thought to correspond to the reality of facts or actions and must be replaced by another theory not before but as soon as this seems to correspond better to reality. Pareto was an enemy of purely negative criticism of imperfect theory, criticism which is useless if it does not help to replace, at least partially, an imperfect theory with another which is less so. Although he paid heed to the criticisms of those who were competent in the field, such as the greatest mathematicians who stimulated him to revise and perfect his theories, he was rarely drawn into directly answering unfounded criticism which started from a non-scientific point of view, that is from experience. When he answered, rather sarcastically, it was from the height of his solid scientific position, thus inducing his adversaries to change their tactics and await a less risky occasion.

Pareto was an enemy of empty thought unconnected to reality. Just as he did not lose himself in vain discussions as, for example, do those scholars who waste time on discussions of methods and terminology which they do not put to use, so he was aware that it was sensible to pose only those problems which he was confident of solving, using the only methods available, however imperfect. This is a canon of scientific modesty which contrasts with sterile presumptuousness. Although it is certainly a vague principle it undoubtedly tends to be violated on occasions by those engaged in the more advanced sciences.

Pareto's unrhetorical style added to the attractions of his writings, where his theories were presented in a scientific form, remarkable for its clarity. This discouraged timewasters from the sort of hermeneutic discussion which takes place around the works of the philosophers who seem to be more appreciated the more hermeneutic they appear, that is, the less the exegetes know what they mean; if the philosophers themselves knew what they meant. Thus, for centuries, even millenniums, discussion has continued and gives cause for meditation and argument for those who do not have more urgent things to examine. This is true of the greater and lesser philosophers of antiquity and proves that these are problems which no one is in a hurry to solve and which can, quite safely, wait all eternity for a solution.

In those works which Pareto wrote in Italian, his language reflects our best traditions, and his style in all his works derives from traditional scientific style based on the classical models of Galileo. These give rise not only to modern scientific style but also to experimental method and modern science.

To conclude these remarks about Pareto's scientific methodology, we may observe that as a past matter in the application of the logical-experimental method to the social sciences he has prepared a sort of catechism of declarations of principle and their application. One could gather and put in order the proposals making a body of precepts of scientific logic or rather scientific philosophy. It was created for the social sciences, but is in the tradition of the best precepts for the more advanced sciences and scientists of Pareto's time. It is therefore valid for all sciences, including the physical sciences which sometimes, recently, have moved into the realm of abstract speculation. These precepts, which should be followed in the sciences in general, have not yet been studied sufficiently in Pareto's works. Any branch of science which came into contact with these precepts would benefit from them, since they would help to avoid error and provide fruitful scientific teaching.

Passing from methodology to results we have to recognise that Pareto has the great merit of having contributed significantly to the advance of economic science from one phase of its development to the successive one. It has progressed from the class of non-mathematical sciences to that of mathematical sciences whose regularities are also determined through analysis. It has advanced, as Croce said of Pareto's economics, to the class of sciences which are sciences, that rigorously solve problems incapable of being solved with equal rigour empirically and determine problems rigorously which can be solved empirically but for whose arithmetic solution in theory the sharpest device of analysis would not suffice.

Following Cournot and Walras, who had paved the way for mathematical economics, Pareto, whose approach unlike that of Walras was purely scientific, brought about significant progress in mathematical economics. Thus he was able to obtain results which were similar to those in mechanics, leading Volterra to call his theory 'analytical economics'. This improvement was all the more remarkable because through it rational economics made further progress and was able to participate in the developments taking place in pure mathematics and other disciplines that use mathematics. Scholars of these disciplines operate in so high a sphere as to be immune from the misunderstandings of the profane and the claims of interest groups. By assiduous common effort and reciprocal exchanges they form the strongest and freest association of minds directed towards scientific progress.

Pareto could not hold the same place in sociology that he held in mathematical economics. Sociology is so much more complex a subject and for this reason is more backward. It was, therefore, not a question of following in the footsteps of economics and moving from a pre-mathematical to a post-mathematical stage. Pareto did not propose to achieve anything of this sort. If anything it was a case of initiating the preparatory stages for a future move.

Pareto made a great contribution to that beginning. He encouraged sociology to develop along logical-experimental scientific lines. He set himself the task of creating a sociology based exclusively on logical-experimental methods and arrived at a point beyond that reached by other sociologists in this field. He did not, however, disregard their scholarship, especially the experimental parts. Some of these sociologists had other non-scientific aims in their study of society while others had been treading the same path as Pareto but with only partial success. Other sociologists thus made a small contribution to the development of experimental theories while others proposed numerous well-known non-scientific theories.

8 In the Decade after his Death

Alfonso de Pietri-Tonelli

Up to this point we have considered the nature of Pareto's thought, his work and his theories, as they appeared in themselves and in relationship to contemporary scientific thought. We have not considered the theoretical schools of thought that began with Pareto nor have we considered the studies carried out on Pareto's work. We have pointed out the effective and, as it were, permanent value of Pareto's theoretical paradigms. We have attempted to give a relevant answer to the question 'was Pareto a great man in his time?'

Now we must go one step further. We must see what additional possibilities there may be, what prospects for Pareto's paradigms.

It is evident that what makes a system of theories great in the long run is its fecundity. A scientist can make a dual contribution, for he can pose and solve certain problems in his lifetime and can also pave the way for the formulation and resolution of other problems at a later date. It is precisely the solving of certain problems which both allows and suggests the positing of others. It is thus that scientific work proceeds in a never-ending progression. Naturally the fecundity of a theoretical system depends not only on the attitudes which are an integral part of the theories, but also on external environmental circumstances, on the existence and abilities of scholars who exploit and develop, sooner or later, the different possibilities embodied in those theories. It is obvious that a system of economic and social theories such as Pareto's would have problems in being an 'open' system, that is one which would open up new perspectives, if the successive period were not conducive to the development of the system. Given that every period has its own unique needs, if in the following period practical values were prized more than theoretical ones, particularly in the social field, the so-called moral sciences will not be able to keep pace with the physical sciences. Thus the fecundity of the system will be a suspended virtue, hidden, at best an indication intelligible at a later time that might be more conducive to the development of the doctrines.

However, it is not possible for us to judge with any degree of certainty the likelihood of further development except on the basis of ascertainable developments later in time.

Thus in order to judge the potential or dynamic value of Pareto's economic and sociological theories (given that the potential value can be considered separately from the real value) one must reply to the question: 'Is Pareto as great in our time as he was in his own?' In order to reply, it is first necessary to examine the characteristics of contemporary scholars and their scientific work, particularly in economics and sociology in order to seek the relationship that exists between these and Pareto.

In so doing (which is not easy in a limited space) we shall intentionally overlook the purely critical literature on Pareto because it is sterile and not worthy of mention. We shall, on the other hand, consider the literature that criticises any gaps in Pareto's theories with the purpose of integrating them, or attempt to go beyond them, surpassing their limits.

Work aimed at perfecting Pareto's theories, stretching them to their limits by developing the principles and thereby paving the way for further developments, must not be underestimated. Above all, the spirit of dissatisfaction with received theories and the desire to react against their passive acceptance are praiseworthy. Such innovative tendencies can lead to important developments. Therefore, we shall not return to that critical literature already mentioned in speaking of Pareto's contributions as a statistician which originated in his empirical law of the distribution of income. We shall, instead, examine two schools of contemporary economic and sociological thought which can be traced back to Pareto and are linked particularly to two of his teachings. The first, characterised by the method he adopted each time he returned to a subject he had studied previously, is that of attempting to further an investigation by considering other aspects, thus refining the treatment. It is in this direction that one of his early doctrines leads, closely connected to both his economic and his sociological theories. Another of Pareto's useful practical teachings is that of following the evolution of the logical paradigms of the most advanced sciences in order to benefit from these in formulating and solving often identical problems in the social sciences. The second school of thought, which deals with his economic theory in particular, can be associated with this teaching. It clearly originates from Pareto's work but attempts to progress beyond it. It is self-evident that these two schools cannot rightly be separated, even though they are of diverse importance, because they are so closely interconnected in the works of the same authors. We shall consider them separately only for clarity of exposition.

In examining the first school, we shall exclude those slavish imitators who have the virtue of preserving the inheritance of Pareto's theory intact but who risk crystallising or mummifying it. Let us, instead, discuss the work of those who develop his theories though without going beyond the general confines of his thought.

Given Pareto's turn of mind and the form of his theories, it was inevitable that his earliest followers and the intelligent propagators of his doctrines would be responsible for revising, controlling, coordinating, and eliminating incompatibilities, while refining and extending the theoretical models in order to introduce other models. This is gradually being done. It is a humble and obscure job compared with the much more brilliant work of those who develop the doctrines using the new mathematical tools to widen their theoretical basis. It must be admitted however, that these are secure steps along old, well-trodden paths, much less risky than those directed along steep and unfamiliar roads. Even the task of giving the finishing touches may pave the way for new developments, from the long-awaited economic statics to economic dynamics. As it continues, this work almost inadvertently surpasses its original boundaries, venturing into new developments perhaps more quietly but no less inexorably.

The work of perfecting and developing Pareto's theories has been conducted above all in economics though to a lesser extent in sociology.

Specific topics have been developed in economics: we cite as an example the work of Barone on the hypothesis of production in a collective state and Sensini's research on rent, which closely followed the methods and principles of the *Cours*. Osorio's research on exchange theory and that of Yntema on the general theory of international trade are two further examples.

There have also been general approaches. As an example let us take Amoroso's lessons, which extended the picture of Paretian economics. He added his own particular mathematical considerations, taking into account the contribution of other mathematical economists, especially Fisher as far as the money market is concerned. Bowley has also made a contribution to mathematical economics in his synthesis which takes into account both the theories of economic equilibrium (Cournot, Walras, Pareto) and the contributions of other writers, especially Anglo-Saxon ones. The scope of our own writings is modest, but we ascribe a great importance to them: that of making Pareto's theories available to university students, thereby resolving complex didactic problems which many authors make the mistake of neglecting. In subsequent studies we have examined elements of economic equilibrium for two subjects and two economic goods and for an unlimited number of subjects and economic goods. Moreover, different economic equilibria and economic movements are considered, re-uniting and coordinating the subjects dealt with in the *Manuale*, in the appendix of the *Manuel*, and in the *Cours*. The subject is treated more synthetically within a general theory of equilibrium of economic change (hypotheses, data, unknowns, equations, results) which by ordering the systems of simultaneous equations, corrects the errors and eliminates the oversights and incompatibilities that become evident as we move from considerations of partial economic equilibrium to those of general economic equilibrium.

In considering all possible different equilibria, this study distinguishes between the position of economic actors and types of behaviour and generalises them so that monopolies and monopolistic advantage constitute specific cases of the general rule. Within these, certain variables have positive values and competition constitutes still other special cases in which these same variables are negated. New hypotheses are posed, such as that of monopolistic advantage, in which any producer can have an advantage as regards any product or factor of production in competition with other producers. The time variable is considered in many cases, as well as specific group political solutions, labour solutions (a political solution to the conflict between maximal individual interests) and corporative solution (political solutions to conflicts of interests between individual producers and an entire group of producers, for example, in the case of the introduction of new distributions of production coefficients). In addition, there are many extensions and specifications as we can see when we move from Walras to Pareto (for example in groups of unknowns – the quantities of each product produced by single producers, the quantities given by single consumers to single producers and vice versa, quantities exchanged by single traders in different economic spheres in the case of any number of actors – of any amount of goods and any number of groups who have different economic equilibria). Thus the way is paved for a greater and more complete synthesis.

We must also remember Bordin's studies in which, among other things, the notion of indices of ophelimity is developed and two types of bartering curves are analysed. Above all, he generalises Pareto's system considering the type of price as an unknown quantity to be determined and introducing the (political) concept of hedonistic drives as necessarily homogeneous and measurable hypotheses represented by vectors that are arranged so as to create resultants. Instead, for planned (guided) economies, (political) indifference curves of community leaders are considered which serve to expand traditional paradigms rendering them appropriate for the study of complex corporative economies. The conditions for international trade are set and the fluctuation of economic activity is always considered since it needs to be accounted for by the theory. It is clear then that the effort to revise Pareto's theories can lead to the extreme limits of his paradigms. Finally, let us recall Weinberger's well-informed manual which develops Pareto's economic theories within the general outline of mathematical economics.

In the field of sociology, Pareto laid the foundations of general sociology which were to be followed by specialised branches. These have been developed in Barone's studies of the economic effect of government taxes, beginning with the economic consideration of the income curve, after which Sensini attempted to formulate general financial problems, following Pareto's directives and treating them as a chapter of sociology. He also attempted to extend Pareto's sociological principles to the study of criminology. Beginning with an outline of the life of social groups, simplified and adapted to the specific needs of the study of economic policy, there has been an attempt to formulate scientifically the study of this discipline, which is of such current interest, interpreting it as a theory of political relations with economic activities. There have been many scholars who have treated economic policy as a kind of applied economics, creating a certain confusion between things which are substantially different. They do not understand that it is preferable to distinguish the actors or groups of actions which are the object of economic studies (free economic actions, connected to individualistic drives) from those that constitute economic policy (political actions, rational or not, which are often compulsory, in that politics means command, coercion and obedience) going back to group drives. Leone constructed a pure theory of politics, developing above all the notion of political types, moving from there to the theory of the state and to different branches of applied politics.

We shall now go on to the second of the two schools of thought that can be connected to Pareto's theories: that which includes the movement towards replacing imperfect theories as well as others that are, or seem to be, less imperfect. It can be easily understood that such a school can only be relevant to the economic and not the sociological theories of Pareto if we avail ourselves of the progress of the logical mathematical methods already in use, their applications to the sciences and the introduction of new calculus and new branches of mathematics. These studies are at the centre of modern scientific thought precisely because they are not simply an end in themselves, but an instrument of progress for the other more advanced sciences.

It is evident that much can be hoped for from such a school of thought although it is certainly not possible to say how certain problems will be solved, nor what will follow when solutions have been found. As in the past, when mathematicians brought rational economics to its present stage of development, it still seems legitimate to expect further progress in analytical economics to come from mathematicians. We cannot deny that Walras was a mathematician who, notwithstanding his limited but admirable mathematical preparation and despite the fact that he drew his inspiration from Cournot, had the inspired idea of applying the equations of mechanical equilibrium to economics. This progress should come in particular from those who, mathematicians at the forefront of mathematical analysis, can easily acquire the necessary knowledge of economics which they might lack. Without such knowledge, the study of mathematics for other purposes of economics could be dominated by purely mathematical considerations instead of mathematics being placed at the service of economics. It is evident that, in economics, one can be an excellent mathematician without being a good economist, whereas the opposite may not be true. A good mathematical economist must be both a good mathematician and a good economist since the real needs of economic theory must not be sacrificed (with hypotheses, etc.) to the theoretical needs of mathematics. There is no doubt that if mathematics is applied to economics, what interests the mathematician may be different from what interests the economist. A mathematician may be interested in certain economic analyses which are of no practical significance and no importance to the economist, while the economist may, instead, be interested in certain mathematical analyses which are of no interest to the pure analyst. For those who study economics without having the delicate tools of mathematics and its latest developments at their command, it is difficult to acquire such knowledge. While they may succeed in doing many other things, it seems highly unlikely that they will make any contribution to pure economics. Thus, if we were to entrust the future of theoretical economics exclusively to them we would be unlikely to see the development we had hoped for. Alas, the future of rational economics would be in jeopardy: the situation would be desperate!

Considering the relationship that necessarily exists between the development of the logical mathematical methods for the sciences and the development of science itself, it can be seen that the period of progress of mechanics, which served as a guide to the other sciences that used it as a model, was contemporary with and successive to the development of infinitesimal calculus.

It is common knowledge that infinitesimal calculus, already systematised in the first quarter of the last century, was perfected during the course of the century. It represented the most delicate and powerful analytical instrument of scientific progress. With the aid of the infinite and infinitesimal it was possible to evaluate finite magnitudes. It provided the analytic means to infer, on the basis of the knowledge of local or instantaneous conditions of a given phenomenon, the integral law of such a phenomenon. It was thus possible to determine elementary laws, using differential equations, and then calculate each element and integrate them. Infinitesimal calculus was the basis, the point of departure for a generalisation that undoubtedly constitutes one of the most brilliant conquests of analysis in the past fifty years.

Following the period of development of infinitesimal calculus and the natural sciences to which calculus is applied, came the period of development of analytical economics which culminated in the work of Pareto.

Cournot's work followed the period in which infinitesimal calculus was systematised and Walras followed Cournot at some distance in time. The work of Vifredo Pareto both overlaps and follows this period of development of infinitesimal calculus.

From the mathematical perspective alone, Cournot, Walras and Pareto belong in an order of progressive development to the same scientific age and to the same historical period of analytical economics. But Pareto was much more fortunate than Cournot and Walras because unlike them, he carried out his work at a time when experimental scientific methods prevailed over abstract principles in the world of science.

We recalled that Volterra had encouraged Pareto's application of infinitesimal analysis to economics. He has also prophesied the application of other branches of mathematics to economics and it so happened that one of the branches of analysis that found application in economics was provided by Volterra himself in the last thirteen years of the nineteenth century.

Volterra, in fact, was responsible both for the formulation and many of the applications of that promising branch of analysis called functional calculus, connected with formal algebra and one of the most perspicacious tools that mathematics has to offer for various applications to problems in the fields of mathematics, mechanics, physics, statistical biology, etc.

Volterra himself observed that classical celestial mechanics and the theories of classical mathematical physics (the propagation of heat, elasticity, optics, electrodynamics), which were constructed according to mechanical models, implicitly presumed, or were constructed as if the present state, that is the initial condition, rigorously determined all the future (which was the only thing considered) of a system. He believed that every event is evident only in the instant in which it occurs, leaving no trace in the future, so that the system does not preserve any memory of the past, that is, of earlier events.

Thus, only one analytical instrument was sufficient for the mathematical analysis of phenomena pertaining to classical mechanics and physics: differential equations. When these became inadequate, partial derivatives could be applied.

Volterra asked himself if natural phenomena manifest themselves following some implicitly acknowledged principle or whether ignoring the heredity of past events is simply an approximation serving to facilitate their study. This happens frequently, for example when considering a phenomenon connected to a finite number of (variable) circumstances, overlooking other infinite circumstances to which it is connected, judging them to be secondary to others that are believed to be primary or preponderant.

It goes without saying that the principle so-called hereditary actions may be open to criticism. Painlevé argued that the only influential actions are those in the present. It can, in fact, be observed that past actions either disappear without leaving a trace or else they do leave a trace in the present. If they leave such a trace, present traces of past events must be included among the actions of the present because such traces of past events constitute present events; they are a present past or what remains of the past in the present. It is in the present that the present traces of past events must be investigated. If it is not possible in the present to understand present traces of past events and the history of this past can be of help, then we must not forget that the construction of past history in order to discover the present is an arbitrary expedient. Volterra, however, with the modesty of the great scientist, being aware of the relative, temporary value of knowledge, believed that the study of the past, even if reduced to a temporary function as a means of understanding the present, can be useful and must therefore be employed. He proved to be right.

The fundamental concept of heredity consists in considering the present condition of a system as depending on its entire previous history, or on the existing traces of its past history; therefore, since time is continuous, the present condition depends on an infinity of variable elements that characterise past events (the existing traces of past events). Thus, previous history can be represented by a quantity that depends on all the values of a function of time, from the present moment to minus infinity or to a past moment prior to which every transmitted event is overlooked. Alternatively it is referred to as a functional of the function of time comprised between the present moment and minus infinity, or the moment preceding which the inherited action is not considered. It can be considered as the function of a line, that is of the curve whose equation is a function of time, considered between the present moment and minus infinity or the moment prior to which every inherited event is ignored; that is, it is the function of the line that geometrically represents the said function.

Volterra admits the basic axiom (that seems to us of a probabilistic nature) of the dissipation of inherited events, for which every inherited event disappears indefinitely in time. He also admits that the existing state depends not on the moment, but only on the history previous to the moment considered.

With the concept of heredity, differential equations and those with partial derivatives are no longer sufficient for the solution of problems, otherwise the initial data would determine the future. Functions that depend on other functions lead to integral equations and integral-differential equations, in which integrals appear that translate the sums of elementary actions corresponding to hereditary actions. They contain the characteristic parameters of the system of time functions during a period preceding the moment considered, up to minus infinity or up to a given moment. More general types of funtional derivative equations have been introduced to express the hereditary action in more general terms which depends on all the values of the function of time in the given hereditary period.

Therefore, the problems of heredity enter into the functional analysis. While the algorithm that governs mechanics and classical mathematical physics is composed of differential equations, the algorithm of mechanics and of hereditary physics is composed of integral-differential equations and of functional calculus. The general equations of hereditary dynamics are, for example, a modification of the classical equations of Lagrange, in order to account for hereditary events.

Hereditary analysis can be applied to all phenomena in which the continuous succession of past states affects future evolution and to all the problems in which the present state, characterised by defined parameters, depends not only on the present value of such parameters, but on all their values in a preceding time interval.

Volterra himself brilliantly proved that the biological phenomenon of the coexistence of different organic species in the same environment has an analogy with hereditary physics in so far as past influences are concerned (that is, inherited actions) and are closely connected to these actions from an analytical perspective. Meanwhile, a group of American mathematicians and European economists, who are the élite of the Econometric Society and its journal, have shown that hereditary methods can also be applied to hereditary economics. These mathematicians and economists form an élite that brings honour to this international association, which I would like to see named after Pareto. By organising frequent meetings of scholars from many countries – who would otherwise be condemned to a sterile soliloquy when the comprehension of their writings requires a certain amount of preparation and effort on the part of the reader – it could bring great honour to analytical economics. These mathematicians and economists showed that hereditary methods can also be applied to hereditary economics. Thus on the basis of new hypotheses, analytical economics can formulate new theorems and achieve what other sciences such as biology have already attained. Hotelling has said that the science of economics that materialises, based on the consideration of maxima and minima, is reduced to a series of problems in the calculus of variations and in the more general theory of the maxima of functionals. It stands in relation to the old theories in the same way as Hamilton's dynamics and the thermodynamics of entropy stand in relation to earlier theories.

Professor Evans, an excellent mathematician, who was for some time a pupil of Volterra, in a treatise that came out after several earlier published essays, emphasises the mathematical character of economics, limiting economic theories to the study of relationships which can be expressed by equations in terms of quantity. After having adopted, in elementary form, the most delicate mathematical tools (calculus of variations and functional calculus), he points out the need for an additional mathematical instrument. From the start he expresses his intention of moving from problems of equilibrium to the study of the so-called processes of economic dynamics, those processes in which, with the passing of time, conditions are modified, so that the time element acquires an important function. As Cournot had done earlier, Evans investigates specific problems. He had already introduced the derivative of price to the equation of demand to account for the influence that the rates of variation and fluctuations in price have on demand. In place of unknown quantities, he considers certain functions of time (dynamic functions) not only as functions of certain quantities and their derivatives with respect to time, within certain limits or beyond such limits (differential linear expressions). These are functions not only of given quantities in a given moment, but of all quantities of an earlier period up to a given moment, quantities which have progressively less intense action with the passing of time (Volterra's functional; linear expression in integrals). The unknowns are determined by rendering these functions maxima or minima and the lapse of time is considered for which certain quantities are a function of other quantities, which are not simultaneous, but belong to an earlier period (of constant duration). Evans considers continuous quantities as functions of discontinuous (periodical) quantities, thereby allowing for economic circumstances which were previously ignored or inadequately accounted for and he attempts to draw closer to reality, by proposing, finally, a concise synthetic general model of economic theory. He hypothesises the economic system as divided into compartments (an economic actor can belong to more than one compartment) and considered the flow of economic goods, including services, through the various compartments, those relating to money being considered as particularly important; lastly, he considers certain characteristic functions which determine the variable functions of the system.

Professor Hotelling, who is also a mathematician, has studied mathematical questions relating to statistics and the economics of taxation; he has contributed to the theory of depreciation (already dealt with by J.S. Taylor) of a machine, demonstrating that the results can be generalised. In addition, he studies stability in the competition between a limited number of competitors and the economics of exhaustible goods.

Professor Roos, who was also a mathematician and a pupil of Evans, has studied economic problems under Evans's guidance. He applied the calculus of variations to the theory of depreciation, studied competition and investigated the function of demand, considering mainly the effects of past prices, of present prices and the expectations of future prices, adopting the theory of integral equations. Since, by definition, an integral is a function of all the points along a curve, the problem of demand is represented by price as a function of time. The author first hypothesises that demand depends on present and past prices and demonstrates that this postulate leads to a functional equation of demand. In the simplest case, that of Volterra's integral equation of demand, the relationship between demand that depends on past prices and price that depends on past demand are identical, due to the reversability of the integral equation. He observes that mathematics has not yet progressed very far with non-linear integral equations, although this is no great cause for concern since it is very likely that the present generation will not exhaust the study of those cases in which linear integral equations are adequate for acceptable generalisations. Considering that present demand is created by a past decision to buy as soon as the means are available, the author observes that many people will buy within a relatively brief period, while others will require more time and some will never be able to buy. This situation can be characterised by assuming that the factors related to the period of time required to transform an earlier decision to buy into actual purchases in the present period, are such that this decision to buy is transformed into actual purchases following a function of Pearsonian frequency of the third type. This assumes that speculative demand depends on expected future prices and that the law of demand, given the common condition of predicting prices a unit of time before the present time interval, consists in a function of the price, a functional of the price and in an expression that implies the derivative of the price in relation to time. Roos also considers time intervals, maintaining that for a functional equation of demand of the type considered, it can be advantageous to find a functional coefficient of the elasticity of demand. He believes that the theory of demand has progressed to a point where further theoretical work can probably not be carried out until necessary statistical investigations have been made to test the value of the hypothesis and the conclusions reached. The author states that this statistical research implies a heavy burden of work; we, however, would say that it is logically impossible. Roos believes that a new type of mathematical statistics is needed in order to carry out such studies, but he states that there is reason for optimism concerning the possibility that statistical laws of demand will be discovered.

Professor Tinbergen introduced the notion of an economic horizon, intended as the period of time in the near future for which an economic actor makes his plans and considers his expectations. The term is imaginative and interesting, but it is not clear how a surface notion can replace in the case of time the notion of a straight line. We already have two directions of the time axis, towards the past and towards the future, starting from the present moment.

Professor Creedy has recently studied the equations of the movements of business activity. Amoroso cautiously followed in the wake of the American mathematicians, making some criticisms of form and one that is not only of form but of substance as well. He observes that it is possible to move on from algebraic equations to differential and functional equations, but it is safer to move ahead by degrees, without making a pause between the transition from algebraic to differential equations; this is already a great step forward. The author uses a linear differential equation of the first order with constant coefficients, which makes the passage to an algebraic equation possible, if time is invariable (a static equation becomes a specific occurrence of a dynamic equation).

These new directions use simple and specific equations of the type developed by Walras and, especially, Cournot, possibly due to the desire for practical verifications which, however, are and will remain strictly impossible, despite progress in statistical surveys and processing. These equations relate primarily to demand, and they could be obtained directly, empirically, if we had the experimental data providing us with curves; however in any case, these would not correspond to the purely economic ones, hypothesised by economic theory. These new directions explore in depth these notions and others, exploiting new instruments of mathematical logic which, yet again, can serve to develop analytical economics.

If parts are separated from the general economic system, they move away from reality in a certain sense; if, instead, we increase our knowledge of these fragmentary aspects of economic reality, they move closer to this reality, gaining in depth at least what they lose in extension and perhaps even more than they lose. More detailed analyses can pave the way to new and better syntheses which, as we have seen, are already being attempted in part. However, bearing in mind the developments in the most advanced sciences, we must remember that in economics the analysis of a specific aspect should not be discouraged; we must not insist that such in-depth studies be of a general nature.

In any case, it cannot be said that the new course in economics is contrary to Pareto's economic theories simply because his was the study of static economics, which does not consider the time variable, whereas the new course is that of dynamic economics, in which economic variables are considered as functions of time. Rather, these new directions and Pareto's economic theories represent two different approaches to economic transformations.

Pareto's economic studies do not consider variables not referring to a certain lapse of time, or as they have been erroneously called, of variables without time. To be precise, Pareto's economic theories hypothesise that certain variable quantities always have the same value for successive time intervals. These variables correspond to given positions of stable equilibrium determined by systems of simultaneous equations that in turn correspond to distinctive moments of time in the process of movements toward and away from similar positions. The successive time intervals correspond to successive identical positions of equilibrium (transformations repeated in time). Pareto assumes quantities that vary around the equilibrium point and from one equilibrium point to another and quantities that vary within finite limits of time, even if they do not appear as explicit functions of time. He affirms insistently that the variable relations of interdependence cannot be considered exclusively as static relations. Going still further, he develops the theory of economic fluctuations that marks the passage from what Pareto himself called dynamics of the first order to dynamics of the second order.

The new course, utilising old as well as new and more appropriate tools of mathematical logic, considers other quantities as variables that can operate or not, treating them as if they operated continually. However these are not the only or even all of the possible variables that could be added. In any case, the new economic theories always consider these variables explicitly as a function of time, within given limits and thus different values must be determined for different intervals of time. Diverse types of variability in time are considered, introducing into the equation variables and derivative of these variables seen in relation to time: variables belonging to a time interval, variables that belong to a different interval (lapse) and variables for the infinite intervals of a limited past or a limited future. The latter serve, above all, to connect the present to the past or to the memory of the past and to future perspectives, thereby creating a dynamic economics, in contrast with an imaginary static economics. This could be called temporal economics, given the importance assumed in it by time functions.

Let us specify that consideration of the past and the future are not new in economics. The one and only novelty of major importance consists in the attempt to use an analysis appropriate to these considerations.

Taking into account the past in economics, we must distinguish whether we are considering objective influences such as stocks or subjective influences of the memory of the past. The consideration of the future is related only to subjective influences (perspectives concerning certain objects).

When subjective influences are considered, particularly of the latter type, we must be careful not to place our illusions in symbols, that is to say, in that which has no practical consistency. It is not easy to establish the point up to which human behaviour is guided in the present by a perspective which in the end has only the present as its basis: where it appears that we are passing from the present to the future, we are merely bringing the future to the present.

*   *   *

In order to develop Pareto's economic paradigms, recourse has been made to certain hypotheses upon which functional calculus is based and to others which produced the calculus of probability.

Thus economic reality has been approached from all sides in the attempt to scrutinise it, starting from an examination of the infinitely small (infinitely small variations) and passing to the infinitely large (large numbers).

The calculus of probability has evolved, giving rise to a new doctrine whose principles are still under discussion, serving to make predictions about chance events, that is, events for which predictions cannot be formulated on the basis of deterministic principles. The initial state, known by the limited number of circumstances that determine it, makes it possible to predict clearly the unknown final state, whether this be one or more than one of the three types of evolution considered by Volterra. These are (1) evolution depending on external circumstances in which all states are determined beginning with an initial state, identified by the sum or integral of an infinite number of instantaneous evolutions; (2) evolution originated by internal circumstances that depends at every instant on the present condition in which all states can be determined, beginning with an initial state, by means of the integration of differential equations; and (3) evolution that depends on all the states that have been passed through (hereditary evolution) in which every state can be determined by means of integral differential equations or functional derivative equations. If, on the other hand, we are dealing with an initial state and we only know that it depends on a large number of unknown or uncertain circumstances, predictions can be made only by means of the statistical principle by which a system, at a given initial moment, is in a certain state, has a certain probability of being in another state in the following moment, and yet another probability of progressing to another state, etc.

The calculus of probability has been useful for those disciplines or parts of disciplines which, not having adopted quantitative methods, had remained behind. These quantitative methods allow only statistical studies of the distribution of mass phenomena or of collectives, for which the action resulting from a large number of variable independent circumstances must be considered (variable according to unknown or unfamiliar laws). In any case, these parameters are too numerous to be considered separately in order to arrive at any kind of regularity, instead of having to consider the action of given circumstances determined with absolute certainty so as to reach regularities, that is, statements of predictable repetitions, which are no longer exclusively statistical.

The calculus of probability provides the theory for the first kind of variables, those of large numbers. They are determined with statistical certainty, relative or practical, considering an extremely likely event as virtually certain. This is of such practical certainty as to satisfy those who formulated the laws of the most advanced sciences. They have always been ready to investigate the circumstances serving to explain the behaviour of reality, which is different from that acknowledged as certain. They have always admitted the possibility of such disavowals, well knowing that what is believed to be certain is no more than highly probable or simply probable. The determinism that intends to provide certainty is based on an audacious and, given our ignorance, illusory assumption. What is certain is at most probable. This brings us to a determination of a statistical type, to a probability that nears certainty.

In any case, probabilistic models have undertaken a function which is analogous and supplementary to that of deterministic models, and no less attractive than these, in the study of complex physical processes. They provide working hypotheses which must be tested by statistical observation. It is only too well known that the first application of probability theory in the physical sciences, which served as a model to the others, was made by Maxwell, the founder of statistical physics, in formulating the law of the distribution of the velocity of gas molecules. Maxwell believed that, confronted with a multiplicity of regulating or disturbing causes of a collision, the effect of chance must prevail over the consequences of dynamic laws so that the vectors of velocity are distributed as vectors representing errors in the position of a point in space.

It is equally well known that in mathematical physics there is an interesting tendency to declare, contrary to classical abstract determinism, a sort of concrete indeterminism that is progressively inclined to admit that all the so-called physical laws are, in the end, laws of probability; they are statistical regularities resulting from numerous observations and only roughly applicable to single observations.

Cournot, who was a master of the calculus of probability, observed that the number of buyers and sellers in a market is sometimes so great as to bring into play the law of large numbers; these can then be mathematically described and serve as the substructure of a mathematical science of economics. Pareto himself observed that, in economics, individual psychology is not studied since the characteristic of this science is the study of large numbers. He considered an average type of economic actor, an average type of economic transformation, etc. He spoke explicitly of a statistical economic equilibrium.

Generally speaking, modern statistical economists are inevitably led to introduce probability in their economic studies. Hotelling and others (Bean, Brown) derived equations of supply and demand functions by means of probability theory. We have seen that Roos relied on a certain type of frequency curve.

Bordin even introduced considerations of probability in Pareto's general economic models. He considered that in social action we can observe not only economic action governed by hedonistic motives, but also economic action whose motives are many and varied. In the present impossibility of applying deterministic principles to such acts, he suggested subjecting them to the laws of probability. Thus for Bordin, trade presents a variety of problems. These are deterministic, as far as certain constraints are concerned, which are expressed by two categories of equations, those of the equality of weighed ophelimity and those of the balance of accounts, and probabilistic as far as others are concerned. These can be expressed by defining, among the infinite possibilities, the most probable distribution, that which corresponds to the maximum probability, and by substituting the third category of Pareto's equations of trade, i.e. those of the balanced accounts of traders, with such a distribution. Thus the principle of the unicity of prices fails because every transfer of wealth implies an individual path followed by a given actor. Thus, Bordin observes, in the equilibrium of gas molecules in a container, the definitive position is known but not the route taken by each one. In reply to the objection that may arise to Pareto's having insisted, as we said earlier, that an income curve is not consistent with a simple probabilistic model, Bordin objects that he has demonstrated, at least as far as trade is concerned, that the curve is consistent with a mixed model.

The value of a mathematical application is essentially the reasoning on which it is based. Hence we must consider as plausible the hypothesis that trade, at least in the case Cournot considered, of a large number of traders and with every possible motive as in Bordin's hypothesis, takes place so as to lead to a casual distribution of goods. Here statistical observation should provide an answer, indicating whether a solution in which chance intervenes only as a disturbing element corresponds better to reality than a solution in which chance intervenes as one of the agent elements, together with other expressly determined ones. Simultaneous economic and extra-economic definitions, with reference to a large number of unknown circumstances must prove compatible at the same time with an economic definition. This definition is given by the equations of preferences which refer back to determined circumstances, known hypotheses and equations which are considered solved at an equilibrium point, the same equations to which are now ascribed time functions. So far the question of distinction, opposition and combination of paradigms or of deterministic or probabilistic factors has not been raised.

In any event, even in the case of the calculus of probability, the methods and the limitations of its use must be examined, but the principle of applying those analyses to economic research that are used in the more advanced disciplines is beyond discussion. The application of such a principle is, in fact, most promising and the highest hopes rest on it.

Those who speak of a crisis in mathematical economics, naturally non-mathematicians, use harsh and irrelevant words which serve only to dramatise what is in reality a guilty conscience. This is due to the fact that they have verified the impotence of current economics which they attempt, in vain, to hide from others. In mathematical economics there is no cause for drama, nor is there any question of crisis. If anything, there is what is called a crisis of development or rather a revision of part of the old principles and the adoption of new ones. We have focused on the need for cooperation among those who adjust old constructions and those who, with the necessary preparation, set about adding new ones.

As for sociology, some time must pass before the present tools of mathematical logic can be extended to this field. Alternatively, new instruments must be created which are more appropriate than those presently available. Although we do not wish to be too optimistic in our forecasts, while at the same time rejecting excessive pessimism, we should recall that Volterra, when creating the instrument for hereditary analysis, believed that its application to the organic sciences was too risky, but only a short time later he himself was to start applying it.

* * *

Both the efforts that are made within the confines of Pareto's economic principles and those made in attempting to surpass them remain abstract speculation and lead, when successful, to theories that fall within the first group of doctrines, that is, those that reflect the highest scientific thought. Other empirical research falls, instead, into the second group, which must be separated from the first because of its different nature and not because it is less important, nor because it is undertaken by different authors.

Evans stated earlier that the overall economic aspect of human work is necessarily too vast a field to be covered by a single theory and concluded that a systematic study of diverse groups of economic conditions is necessary in order to establish hypotheses that distinguish the different groups. More recently, he observed that a large number of simultaneous equations with a large number of unknowns can serve to express a theory that cannot be adequately expressed in words and he provides no opportunity for a numerical control. Pareto has already made an often-cited observation of this sort.

The major complication which appears in moving from Walras's equations to those of Pareto and others, seems a flaw to those who are in search of controls, which are in large part illusory: such people are thus induced to return to Walras and Cournot. However, in reality, it is a merit if, like Pareto, one is primarily seeking a synthesis of the operation of concrete economic systems through the use of general equations or, in other words, of the connections existing between all quantities and the means of determining values of different categories of interdependent variables, not only of those which seem to have greater importance in determining certain circumscribed problems. These are studied by removing them from social reality and then separating a part of this same economic reality from the remainder of economic reality, disregarding both the relationship between the economic reality that has isolated and the rest of economic reality and the relationship between these and the remainder of social reality.

Evans admits that there are two possible ways to acquire information. The first applies statistical methods to determine averages or sums that have significant relationships with the system under consideration. The second is a system that consists of only a few variables, subject to relationships suggested by experience.

These two methods of controlling theories, however, are evidently arbitrary. Both are abstractions of reality (just as is any theory or any form of scientific thought) which, ultimately, are the same thing, even when the modality of application is different. They compare a statistical abstraction with an analytical abstraction. In the first case, averages or sums of many parameters are considered. In the second, only a few parameters are considered in isolation. In any case, economic theory is not to be compared with economic reality because there is no economic reality separate or concretely separable from social reality. Pareto wrote that he did not believe that either applied economics or economic dynamics or any other similar study can lead us to the discovery of the nature of concrete phenomena. In order to attain this knowledge, the study of sociological synthesis is indispensable, but it is evident that even this cannot go beyond certain limits. The two methods directed at increasing our knowledge of economic life are expedients justified by the fact that, if we want to control economic theories, being unable to do so experimentally we can only opt for one of the above two methods. The second is evidently more manageable and less likely to create illusion and is, therefore, preferable.

Alongside the two previously mentioned methodologies, two empirical-statistical methods can be considered, even if the first is ostensibly an intermediate solution between pure general theory and simple empirical research. It attempts to apply statistics to general economic problems, while the second attempts instead to apply statistics to more specific economic problems, although these distinct branches of research may often be conducted by the same authors.

We must remember that the tendency, on the one hand, to carry out general scientific investigations and, on the other, to turn one's attention to specific studies, recurs throughout the brief history of mathematical economics, according to the varying inclination of scholars. In fact, after Cournot, who was interested in empirical tests, two abstract tendencies emerged: a general one, as with Walras, and a more specific one, as with Marshall. Pareto's very general analyses followed that of Walras while the detailed research carried out by Fisher and others followed Marshall. At present, in the same empirical statistical field the two tendencies still exist, those influenced by the more general equations of Walras and those going back to Marshall's more specific research into supply and demand.

As an example of the first type of research, we shall survey the so-called synthetic economics of Moore.

Moore affirms that Cournot was following a route which could lead from the theory of probability to numerical applications, but then he abandoned the idea of concretely determining the conditions of general equilibrium. He erroneously believed that the only certain means possible of comparing theory with reality is by statistical empirical research which, however, on account of its methodology, is of no greater value than any other. Moore further states that Walras and Pareto remained abstractly theoretical, avoiding confrontation with reality. Their followers condemn their attempts in this direction. In order to reconcile the real with the rational, using recent statistical methods, synthetic economics considers the general equilibrium that is created by the economic forces presently operating in our ever-changing economy. Moore postulates that such an equilibrium tends to converge along the lines of general trends of diverse economic factors and he abandons the axiom of absolute free competition in favour of the Aristotelian premise that businessmen operate in the direction that will bring them the greatest profit. Among the conditions that determine shifting equilibrium, Moore separates the empirical from the rational. The empirical elements are the laws of demand, laws of supply and the coefficients of production. All these elements are empirically determined by the new axioms. The rational elements include the foregoing premises and their consequences when they are applied deductively to empirical elements. If the premises are appropriately chosen and the empirical elements are adequately evaluated, then, the author affirms, the logical consistency of the rational construction should guarantee the final agreement between the probable frequencies of empirical events.

Moore claims that all the interdependent economic quantities are presented in a synthesis of simultaneous equations which he says are real. The equations have concrete statistical forms in order to express trade, production, capitalisation and distribution with all the variable functions of time. He then goes on to say that the problem is solved by applying the mathematical method when there are as many independent equations as there are unknown quantities, whereas with the synthetic method that is only half the solution. After presenting abstract simultaneous equations, it must be proved that the same equations can be derived empirically and that a real solution to the problem is possible. The advantage of the synthetic method is, according to the author, that it fuels the hope of introducing rational forecasts in economic life (which are, by rule, impossible) and illuminating controls which, at best, are difficult. This is because, Moore says, from the study of simultaneous equations that determine shifting equilibrium, the possible sources of fluctuations can be localised by means of successive approximations, starting from the most important source. The author finds algebraic forms for the three groups of functions considered and adapts them to empirical data. Thus he arrives at three groups of real functions: demand, supply and coefficients of production.

In order to go from Walras's general static equilibrium (the empiricists always lead back to Walras) to a general shifting equilibrium, each of Walras's four groups of equations is replaced by a group of statistically verifiable equations that can be applied to the present variable economy. In place of Walras's demand equations there are concrete demand equations which reproduce the partial elasticity of demand as constants, or as linear functions of their respective price or as quadratic functions of the price. In place of Walras's supply equations there are concrete supply equations which reproduce the partial elasticity of supply as constants or linear functions of their respective prices or as quadratic functions of prices. In place of the constant coefficients of production by means of which Walras expresses the equations of supply and demand, there are concrete variable coefficients of production, in which the partial derivatives relative to production are themselves reproduced as constants, as linear functions of their respective factors of production, or as quadratic functions of these. In place of Walras's equations of cost and price which depend on the postulate of constant coefficients of production, other equations are substituted which contain real coefficients of production.

These four groups of equations, Moore writes, like those of Walras, determine general equilibrium, but a real as opposed to a hypothetical equilibrium (we must, however, first agree on the meaning attributed to such adjectives), a shifting as opposed to a static equilibrium. According to the author, this is a shifting equilibrium around the lines of general trends.

With eight groups of equations similar to those preceding, Moore determines general mobile equilibrium, considering capitalisation. By substituting concrete dynamic functions, as he calls them, for the static functions of Walras, the author extends Walras's analysis of the fluctuations around a static equilibrium to the description of concrete fluctuations around a general shifting equilibrium. He examines the eight groups of equations in order to indicate the sensitive points at which the oscillations, understood as complete fluctuations of an economic quantity around its position of normal equilibrium, originate.

As is evident, this is a statistical conception, an attempt to shorten the distance between theory and reality statistically, to give a statistical equilibrium to the movement of economic transformations. Even if we move from the theoretical consideration of individual actions providing suggestions for general discussion to the consideration of statistical averages of individual actions, it is nevertheless an abstract manner of conceiving and defining economic reality. We give statistical investigation, capable of indicating the form of the parameters of equations of economic equilibrium, an excessively arbitrary task: that of providing these very same parameters. We do not wish to repeat our objection that empirical curves can be interpolated advantageously whereas they cannot be extrapolated without serious risks (since, as a rule, they tell us very little about the future). However, it must be emphasised that empirical curves, in so far as they correspond to reality, represent the results of economic and extra-economic acts that are conveniently disregarded by the theory, while so-called synthetic economics must abandon this rational principle. It remains to be seen whether there are, in effect, advantages to this rational-empirical union, advantages which consist in an approach to reality and the possibility of further developments in economic research. Finally, does all this make up for what is lost in terms of rigour and penetration in theoretical analysis and for the hindrance to further analytical developments?

Going on to examine specific statistical research in economics, it is soon evident that it is connected to noteworthy methodological developments as well as to statistical surveys and has been the source of many important contributions in these two fields.

Evans himself designed a research project which bordered on general research, directed at bringing theory closer to statistically observable economic reality; it concerned the specific statistical research which we shall now discuss.

Evans attempted to introduce what he called comprehensive variables into economic theory and to see whether a theory could be constructed in terms of only a few general variables such as the production of capital per unit of time, or the use of capital and labour per unit of time, or the production of goods for direct consumption per unit of time. He then noted that quantities such as the first and the last do not, in fact, exist because they are hypotheses composed of different goods each of which must be considered as having a different size. Similar considerations must be made for different prices. In order to apply quantitative analysis to these quantities, the author considers them as indices of business and of prices for groups of goods and services within the specified classes.

It is obvious that the same considerations that apply to Moore's theories are valid for Evans's work.

The measurement of the final degree of utility falls within the category of specific statistical research. These studies attracted Pareto himself at the outset and he seemed to nourish some hope of possible practical applications, but he later wrote that research of the type carried out by Fisher should be abandoned. Such research, however, was later taken up by Fisher and by Frisch, who wrote several articles as well as a book.

In this connection it can be observed that elementary ophelimities are connected to individual feelings which are not comparable between individuals and cannot be reduced to quantitative expressions: they can be subjected to the arithmetic of addition and division, calculation of averages, etc. (with their properties) which are not directly measurable. Those which are referred to as measurement of elementary ophelimities are at best measurements obtained indirectly by means of quantitative manifestations open to statistical surveys and to the calculation of averages: they are abstractions referring back to statistical surveys of the behaviour of particular groups of individuals who are not motivated by purely economic considerations.

Fisher's studies fall within the framework of specific research in the monetary field.

Professor Amoroso, on the basis of Fisher's and Keynes's work, in his later writings on mathematical theories, treated monetary dynamics as a resultant of different kinds of reciprocal actions and reactions, both spontaneous (i.e. inertia) and induced (mechanical and directive) in the industrial, commercial and banking systems. He attempted to study actions and their successive reactions, not those resulting from individual enterprise, but global and therefore statistical actions. These global actions were studied in place of the simultaneous reciprocal actions of different units, parts of economic systems and different individual systems which all form the general system. Amoroso studied, from an empirical statistical point of view, the movements of derived indices (derivatives of indices with regard to time) as representative of the actions of the specific systems of industry, commerce and banking. He also considered the movements that, in their possible combinations, lead directly to primitive indices as expressions of corresponding reactions. He formulated equations which he termed equations of commerce, banking and the workshop and which are based on direct or inverted correlations of movements, from these he arrives at three homogeneous differential equations with constant coefficients which make up a system that, according to him, is representative of the general dynamics of circulation and with which he attempts to explain so-called cyclical movements.

Statistical research on the laws of demand and the flexibility of demand refer back to the same sources. Several scholars, including Professor Schultz, have dedicated themselves to this type of research.

Studies of the different types of economic fluctuations also go back to the same roots. Pareto had been involved in similar research that gave birth to a vast quantity of literature – statistical, methodological and applied – by Mitchell among others, and Bordin's research on the methodology of seasonal fluctuations. In general, the literature on economic fluctuations now seems to be in a phase of critical revision of the fundamental hypotheses of the studies and of their relative methodologies, trying to find those which are most appropriate. Many illusions no longer exist: they were part of an early enthusiasm for periodic regularity, prediction and the separability of the different kinds of movements.

We wish to recall that we, too, have carried out numerous systematic statistical studies in our laboratory. The most recent concern the relationship between the trends of economic, demographic and fiscal data, the relationship between prices and production, prices and commercial sea freight, prices and unemployment, prices and bankruptcy, prices and public budgets and studies of disagreement in inverse exchanges, prediction of runs on the stock market, the era of gold coins and that of paper money, railways and economic trends, the international wine economy, etc.

We have seen that Pareto contributed to the development of statistical methodology and its applications. However, he never forgot the contrast that exists between the rigour of the formulas of mathematical statistics and the imperfect, approximative nature of the data that statisticians must necessarily adopt. He was never under the illusion that economic science can be created on a purely statistical basis, even if he nourished excessive hopes about the role in economics of empirical laws drawn from statistics. These empirical laws serve to test already established theoretical laws and to discover new ones. This is a more realistic attitude, more appropriate to the understanding of the role of statistical research in the construction of economic theories.

Apart from the fact that a good statistician is not always a good economist, the science of statistics can detect and reveal only certain aspects of economic and social reality. Rational economics, instead, considers all the economic aspects of concrete economic and social reality which cannot be reduced to economic analysis or mere statistical investigation. Pareto allowed himself to be enticed by a hybrid approach such as that arising from the desire to conduct the results of empirical statistical investigations within the confines of the formulas of analytical economics.

Considering the general nature of the new analytical and empirical statistical tendencies, it can be seen that they all have something in common: the intention of utilising in the study of economics the resources of mathematical analysis, including statistics, as do the other sciences, particularly the physical mathematical sciences.

None of these developments would have been possible without the work of earlier economists and mathematical statisticians, among whom Pareto occupies an eminent position. Without Pareto, quantitative economics would not be what it is today, nor would it hold such promise for the future. The contributions made to analytical economics after Pareto are of little importance in comparison to the work he carried out: its form today derives principally from his theories.

A more thorough study of all of Pareto's works is advisable for scholars in the field and would illustrate how difficult it is to open up new and certain paths in economics. Since Pareto had a thorough understanding of the different branches of mathematics and their applications to the other sciences, he travelled or at least attempted many roads, and ingeniously anticipated many new directions. We must admit that the study of Pareto's theories still leaves much to be desired: they have not been as widely and systematically studied as other classics of economics. Even highly esteemed scholars of mathematical economics have recently shown that they are unfamiliar with some of Pareto's important theories.

Notes

FOREWORD

1. Max Weber, *The Protestant Ethic and the Spirit of Capitalism*, Allen & Unwin, 1930.
2. V. Pareto, 'Un applicazione ai teorie sociologiche', *Revista italiana di sociologia*, 1901, pp.402–56; *Les Systèmes socialistes*, Paris, vols I and II, 1903 (reprint 1926). In these works Pareto asserted that the culture of socialism had a major influence on human ethos, passions, instincts, feelings and will-power, serving as a catalyst for social change.
3. J.A. Schumpeter, *Capitalism, Socialism and Democracy*, London: George Allen & Unwin, 1943.
4. 1916, 4 vols, Florence: Barbera. Translated into English by A. Bongiorno and A. Livingston as *The Mind and Society*, London: Jonathan Cape, 1935.
5. *The Mind and Society*, vol. II, p.519.
6. *Ibid.*
7. *Ibid.*
8. *The Rise and Fall of Elites*, p.100. Pareto believed that socialism was a religion with a greater element of rationality than Protestantism. He wrote: 'many people imagine that they can effectively combat socialism by combating the theories of Marx, just as others believed it possible to combat Christianity effectively by pointing out scientific errors of the Bible. There are few educated people today who would not recognize those errors. And yet, what damage has it done to Christianity? None.' So, to put it in Weberian terms, if Catholicism and Protestantism have a different ethos, so too is the ethos of Protestantism and socialism.
9. J.A. Schumpeter, *The Economics of Sociology of Capitalism*, edited by R. Swedberg, Princeton University Press, p.288. However, as is found in this volume, both de Pietri-Tonelli and Bousquet conclude that Pareto is *not* a socialist.
10. *The Mind and Society*, vol. IV, p.1549.
11. *Op. cit.*, p.1552.
12. Schumpeter, *op. cit.*, p.124.
13. *Op. cit.*, p.256.
14. *Op. cit.*, p.124n.
15. M. Morishima and G. Catephores, *Value, Exploitation and Growth*, McGraw-Hill, 1978.
16. At least in as far as can be seen in his *Capitalism, Socialism and Democracy*, p.236.
17. J.R. Hicks, 'Pareto Revealed', *Economica*, pp.318–22, a book review of *Lettere a Maffeo Pantaleoni da Vilfredo Pareto* , 3 vols, ed. G. de Rosa, Banka Nazionale del Lavoro, Rome, 1960.

118   *Notes*

1 A SHORT BIOGRAPHY

1. The chair of political economy at the University of Lausanne, Switzerland.

2 THE ECONOMIST

1. The term 'ophelimity' was used by Pareto to describe the capacity that makes something satisfy a need or desire, whether it is legitimate or not.

4 PARETO AND SOCIALISM

1. The extract, *Marxisme et économie pure*, is available from Droz, Genoa (1966).
2. Editor's note: See p.44.
3. Another writer of this period, Villaumé, accords humanity three types of natural rights entirely different from those of Fourier.
4. However, in our view, not all of the Marxist theory of interest is therefore to be dismissed, its sociological aspect in particular warranting consideration. See our 'Observations sur la théorie de l'intérêt', *Revue d'économie politique*, 1927, no.5.
5. See our *Evolution sociale aux Pays-Bas*, p.123n.
6. See *Is*.
7. We are describing an objective phenomenon. In fact, the new élite nearly always acts in good faith.
8. 'Um applicazione di teorie sociologiche', *Rivista italiana di sociologia*, July 1901, pp.402–56.
9. Editor's note: That is, chapter II of Bousquet's book, *Vilfredo Pareto, sa vie et son oeuvre*, which is not included in the present volume.

5 THE SOCIOLOGIST

1. See note 9 of the previous chapter.
2. Editor's note: Combinations of every possible kind are covered by this. Later, Bousquet discusses Pareto's comments on the ability to perceive and make use of certain combinations as a means to successful business enterprise. Another aspect is the way certain people combine in conspiracies and government intrigue, a matter of great interest to Pareto and also commented on later by Bousquet.
3. It is as well to recall here his minor monograph *Le Mythe vertuiste et la littérature immorale*. It does not have great theoretical significance. In the last chapter, however, Pareto, moving from the subject in question to general

theory, shows once again the necessity of studying the sentiments of societies and not the derivations arising from them. The *Mythe* gives clear evidence of Pareto's wide literary knowledge. In particular he quotes from the writers of ancient Greece with a rare confidence. His thesis is as follows: those who attempt to rid society of immoral literature are working in vain, since the tendencies on which this literature is based is too firmly rooted in human nature. Furthermore, the 'virtuists' [moralists] are themselves driven by the sexual residue. Their fanaticism is similar, in certain respects, to religious fanaticism. Finally, history shows very clearly that the most eminent men and the most powerful nations were not necessarily the most virtuous; quite the contrary.

4. The great interest of this theory is that through it we can understand, by means of deduction, what Pareto stated after his analytical studies, and thus understand increasingly well that the actual structure of society is a great deal less variable than its external form, perceived only through such things as political, social or other theories, would suggest.

    This is why, when one sets aside these things in order to concentrate on states of mind, certain analogies in society appear, at first glance, to be very dissimilar. But this is not one of the least curious aspects of Pareto's sociology. To the countless examples which the writer gives, we will add two others: (a) it is sometimes asked how an institution such as the *Inquisition* could be accepted since it led to the condemnation of innocent people, a situation likely to shock people's feelings. If the answer is that it continued to exist owing to the veneration accorded to this [church] institution (a second class residue), one would understand. But one can go further: today, the jury system produces scandalous decisions resulting in the acquittal of people who are clearly guilty, having confessed to their crimes. Though not a divine institution, the jury is for many people to be revered, because it expresses 'the will of the people'. 'Derivations' have changed: once theological, they are today democratic, But the basis remains the same. This is all the more true in that, given the existence of hypersensitivity and the general undermining of punishments, sentiments should not be more shocked in the Middle Ages by the condemnation of an innocent than they are by the acquittal of the guilty today. Our observation is objective and is neither an attack on, nor a defence of the jury system.

    (b) It will be asked how a people as rational and positive as the Romans could believe in soothsayers in spite of the innumerable confutations experienced. Today one would say that a similar turn of mind would be unthinkable. However, we do not know whether two journalists can look at each other without laughing, but we do know very well that there is not one iota of agreement between their positions about the beginning of an undertaking, be it political, military, financial, colonial, or diplomatic, nor about the eventual destination of society. *A priori* one journalist is not more likely to make correct predictions overall than any other if, for example, one brings to mind all that the various journalists predicted during the last war. The analogy can be taken further. The haruspices knew, in order to please those in power, how to give favourable predictions for any given enterprise. To summarise, soothsayers and journalists have many more psychological similarities than would appear at first sight.

In the whole of this section of *Sociologie*, Pareto studied many other subjects indirectly, but in great detail; we will simply refer to his critique of animism, totemism, etc.

5.   In *Cours*, 619–29, Pareto wrote the following which seems very accurate: 'The comparison with a system based on material factors is, in our view, the only one which can help us to understand the highly complex interaction of social phenomena, and consequently give us a clear idea of economic and social equilibrium. Furthermore a materialistic system lends itself to observations of *virtual movements*... Conversely, the comparison with a living organism is the best when it is a question of forming an idea of the evolution of society. Mechanistic systems offer us little or no illumination on the growth and evolution of social organisms.' This less dogmatic concept of the socio-economic equilibrium seems to me the best.

6.   We have used this theory in our *Evolution sociale aux Pays-Bas* (last chapter).

7.   Editor's note: Pareto suggests elsewhere that it would be helpful to think of '*R*' as standing for '*rentiers*' and '*S*' as standing for 'speculators' – or, rather, that the term 'speculators' could be used for members of category *S* and the French term '*rentiers*' could be used for members of category *R*.

8.   *Rivista italiana di sociologia*, March 1917.

9.   Quoted by Rosak in 'Chaleur et industrie', *Revue de l'industrie du Feu*, June 1923.

10. However, the composer of *Fairies* (and even of *Rienzi*) did also compose *The Ring of the Niebelungen*.

11. I should add that at the time I knew Pareto's system less well than today.

6 PARETO AND THE PROBLEMS OF MODERN SOCIETY

1.   See *inter alia* the curious article 'Due uomini di stato' by Giolitti and Lloyd George, *Ronda*, July 1921.

2.   In a subsequent passage, he showed that the reasons invoked by Germany for its violation of Belgian neutrality were identical to England's reasons for seizing the Danish fleet. It is clear that this method of studying history is more effective than the one which consists of extracting moral lessons!

3.   See our *Restauration financière de l'Autriche*, the last chapter.

4.   Concerning Pareto's influence on Fascism, see V. Beckerath, *Wesen und Werden des Faschistisches Staates*, p.43. The statement that Mussolini knew Pareto at Lausanne, and above all was one of his students may be true, but I do not think so.

5.   This can mean that:

(1) the innumerable derivations used by the current leadership in Italy are admirable and marvellous; the government's intrigues, which are at least part of the reason for its continued hold on power, should be taken seriously; one can approve of the countless persecutions, injustices, abuses of power, and tyranny of all sorts in the government's treatment of its enemies. In other words, this form of government is deemed to be perfect.

(2) taking full account of the above-mentioned facts, it is believed that the current leadership has saved the country from anarchy, and in many respects has accomplished a national revival that is both effective and lasting.

(3) quite apart from the benefits to Italy, Fascism is the sole expression in Europe of the sentiments needed by the bourgeoisie and capitalist civilisation, and thus alone capable of forming an effective bulwark against socialism and Bolshevism.

Had Pareto lived longer, he would certainly have been a 'Fascist' in the sense of 2 and 3. We also would describe ourselves as such in terms of 3. It will be asked how it is possible to reconcile this stance with a scrupulous objectivity in sociology, political economy, etc. The answer is very simple. The facts included in categories 1, 2, and 3 will always exist, irrespective of any value-judgement attached to them. Therefore, they can be analysed in a rational and scientific way. Then, one is free either to accept or reject them. One can prefer pears to apples, or vice versa, and at the same time study pear and apple trees dispassionately.

6. See amongst others, Pareto's obituary in *Avanti!*, and the interview with him in *Secolo* (16 November 1922) ('I am a scholar, present at the field of action, observing what happens. Now that everyone has become a friend of the Fascists, I will refrain from expressing an opinion on current events. I have never liked – and will always dislike – being part of the clamorous chorus of eulogists.') Likewise, in the letter which he wrote to M. Zuccharini, editor of *Critica politica*, part of which was included in his obituary on 25 September 1923, Pareto revealed himself to be every bit as reserved as he was in his correspondence with me on the same subject.

7. See the previously mentioned article in *Critica politica*.

8. See in particular, his study 'Il Fascismo' (*Ronda* 15 January 1922), in which he concluded that Fascism was possibly a 'sign of the major trends in social evolution'. This is hardly meaningful! See also his article in *Rivista d' Italia* 13 April 1922 on predicting social phenomena.

9. 'Since I am neither a socialist nor a cleric, I have always defended the liberty of both groups', *Journal des économistes*, 15 May 1900 ('The Socialist Threat').

10. See also *Giornale economico*, January 1923, and *Secolo*, 17 May 1923: 'To exercise power with moderation is to draw near to perfection. This is what Augustus knew how to do', etc.

11. It seems that his articles in *Naçion* are even more explicit.

12. Editor's note: Pareto means by this the increasing rigidity of society as social mobility decreases.

13. We can see in *Cours* 690ff. the first signs of the idea which we are discussing now.

7 FASCISM AND THE IMPARTIAL THEORETICIAN

1. Throughout this speech the terms 'hereditary' and 'heredity' are used in the following sense: 'The fundamental concept of heredity consists in considering the present condition of a system as depending on its entire previous history, or on the existing traces of the past history.'

Index

academic freedom 72
aggregations 47
Amoroso, L. 93, 102, 113–14
Andler, Ch. 31
Antonines 62
aristocracies 38–9
Aristotle 34, 50, 110
Arrow, K. xviii
asceticism 18, 48
astrology 87
astronomy 41
Athens 43, 65
Augustine, Saint 46
Augustus 53, 64, 69, 71, 121n
Austria 62

banks 7, 77, 113–14
Barone, E. xxi, 93, 95
Bastiat, F. 32
Beckerath, V. 120
Belgium 65, 120n
Berthollet, Pierre 57
biology 5, 8, 16, 41, 84, 100
  hereditary 84
  statistical 97
Bolshevism 62, 69, 80, 121n
Bongiorno, A. 117
Bordin, A. 94, 106–7, 114
Bousquet, G. 118
Bossuet, Jacques 55
bourgeoisie 39, 68, 121n
Bowley, A.L. 93
Britain xv
  see also England
Brunetiere, Vincent de Paul 35
business cycles 12–13

Caesar, P. 69, 71
calculus 16, 83, 84, 85, 95
  differential 83
  functional 83, 85, 97, 99, 100, 104
  infinitesimal 10, 83–6, 96–7
  of probability 85, 104–7
  of variations 100, 101
capital 32, 54, 113
Capital (Marx) 29

capitalisation 7, 111, 112, 117n, 121n
capitalism xx, xxii–xxiii, xxiv, 54
Carlyle, T. 31
Carnavon, Lord 43
Catephores, G. 117
Catholics 71
Catiline 63, 69
Cauchy, A. 10
chance events 104–5, 107
chemistry 8, 41
Christianity 71, 117n
class struggle 35
coalitions 7
Coenobium 66
combination (innovation) 16, 62
communism 2, 36, 69
competition xxi, 7, 9, 21, 22–7, 77, 94,
  101, 110
Comte, A. 34–5, 50
Condorcet, Marquis de 50
consumption 7, 113
corporatism 80, 81
Cournot, Antoine 6, 9–10, 21, 22, 76, 86,
  89, 93, 96, 97, 100, 102, 106, 107, 108,
  110
Cours d'économie politique (Pareto)
  1896 2, 4, 5, 6–11, 13–14, 16–17, 21, 24–
  5, 41, 52, 75–6, 82, 86, 93, 94, 120n, 121n
Creedy, Professor 102
criminology 95
Croce, B. 10, 20, 89
crystallisation 72–4
Curbastro, Professor 83
currency devaluation 66, 68
customs duty 76
cycle of demogogic plutocracy 18, 62–4,
  69–72

Debreu, G. xiv, xviii
deductive system 50
defeatism 64
demagogic plutocracy 62–3, 69, 72
demand 100, 110, 114
  function of 101–2, 106, 111
democracy 2, 18, 47, 64, 78
depreciation 101

123

derivations xviii, 15–18, 31–2, 37, 40, 44,
    45–53, 55–7, 59, 61–2, 67, 71, 119n
determinism 86, 105–7
de Rosa, G. 117
dictators 71
distribution 7, 33, 38, 107, 111
    of wealth 33–4, 38

Eastern Europe xiii, xxiv
Econometric Society xxvi, 99–100
economic actions xii–xiv, xvii
economic behaviour 14–15, 41
economic dynamics 93, 100, 103–4, 109
economic equilibrium xi, xiii, 6–8, 9–10,
    21–8, 41–2, 57–8, 93–4, 106
equations 7, 10, 21–8, 111–12
economic evolution 55
economic fluctuations 7, 14, 17, 94–5, 103,
    114
economic horizon 102
economic paradigms 91–5, 104–8
economic phenomena 14, 41, 55–7, 61–2, 66
economic prosperity 61–2, 66, 73
economic reality 7, 57, 103, 104, 109, 112,
    115
economic research 6–15, 108–15
economic statics 93, 103–4
economic systems xiii, 7, 101, 109, 113
economic theories, schools of thought
    from 91–6
economic utility 7, 9
economics xi–xiii, 59, 82, 87–8, 92
    analytical 90, 96, 97, 100, 103, 115
    applied 7, 95, 109
    comprehensive xiv, xvii–xx, xxvi
    hereditary 84, 99–100
    mathematical 2, 5, 7–12, 19, 89–90, 93,
        96, 100, 106–10, 115
    pure xviii, 7, 42, 50, 52, 55, 57, 96
    rational 8, 9, 10, 82–3, 86, 90, 96, 115
    schools of 1, 5–6
    synthetic 110–12
    temporal 104
    theoretical 77
Economie Journal (de Foville) 29
economists, classical 6, 41
Edgeworth, Francis 6, 9
Einstein, Albert 83
Eléments d'économic politique pure (Walras)
    1900 10, 21
élites xvii, 38–9, 69–70, 74
    circulation of xxii–xxiii, 14, 55–6, 58–9,
        61–2

Encyclopédie des sciences mathématiques
    (Pareto) 1911 3, 4, 5, 6
Engels, F. xii, 35
England 39, 58, 64, 120n
entrepreneurs xiv–xv, xx
equations 7, 10, 16, 21–8, 94, 97, 99,
    101–5, 107, 108–12, 114
Europe xiii, xxiv, 61–3, 65, 68–9, 74, 121n
    see also specific countries
Evans, G.C. 100–1, 108–9, 112–13
evolution 17, 55–6, 105
exchange 8, 21, 52, 93

family 47
Fascism xxv, 2, 19, 62, 69–72, 79–81,
    120–1n
fatal progress 17
Fatti e Teorie (Pareto) 1920 3, 4, 14, 64,
    65, 67
feminism 74
Ferrara, F. 2, 3, 6, 76
fiction residue 57
First World War 12, 64–6, 67–8
Fisher, I. 6, 9, 93, 110, 113
Flaminius, Gaius 66
force 17, 53–4, 62–3, 69, 70, 73, 79, 80
Fourier, F. 31, 35, 118n
France 37, 62, 65, 71
free competition 7, 21, 22–7, 110
free credit 32
free trade 21, 76
freedom 76, 78
freedom of the press 71–2
French Revolution 61
Frisch, R. 113
fund for wages 33

Galileo 85, 89
general equilibrium theory xi, xxiv–xxv,
    8, 110
geometry 8, 9
Gerarchia 69, 70, 72
Germanic countries 49
Germany 62, 64, 65, 67–8, 120n
Gide, C. 29, 31
Giolitti, G. 20
Giornale degli economisti xxi, 4, 75
Giornale d'Italia 65, 71
Giornale economico 71, 121n
Gossen, H.H. 41, 43
governments 17, 53–4, 63, 65–6, 69–70,
    71–3, 77, 80, 95
Greece xxii, 36, 63, 66, 119n

Hahn, F. xiv, xviii
Hamilton, W.R. 100
hereditary actions 98–100, 108
hereditary economics 84, 99–100
hereditary mechanics 83–4
heredity 98–9, 105
Hicks, J.R. xiv, xxv
historical materialism xi, xiii, xvii
history 17, 18, 42, 53, 64, 66–7, 71, 73, 78, 98–9
Hitler, Adolf 80
Homo œconomicus 42
Hotelling, Professor 100–1, 106
human action xxi, 15, 17, 19–20, 43, 82–3
humanitariansim 38, 62, 70, 78
hysteresis 84

ideology xiii, 55
Il mito virtuista e la letteratura immorale
   (Pareto) 1914 3, 4, 13, 18
income 7, 54
   distribution of 11–12, 92
income curve 10–11, 38, 95, 107
inductive method 43
Industrial Revolution 58
industry xxii–xxiii, 72, 113–14
inflation 2
inheritance 33
instinct for combinations xx, xxii–xxiii,
   16, 17, 45–7, 62–3
instinct for group-persistence xx, xxi–xxiii
integral-differential equation 99
integrity of the individual xx, 16, 48–9
interest 55
international trade 7, 9, 77, 93, 94–5
interventionism 2, 76
isophelime 9
Italian Association for the Advancement of
   Science xxiv
Italy 1–2, 69–71, 78–9, 120–1n

Jevons, W.S. 6, 41
justice 47, 48–9

Keynes, J.M. 113

labour xxiv, 33, 113
Labriola, Arturo 35–6
Lagrange, J. 99
laissez faire economic policy 76, 80
Latin countries 49
Lausanne school 10
Le mythe vertuiste et la littérature immorale
   (Pareto) 1911 3

League of Nations 67
Lenin, V.I. 71
Les systémes socialistes (Pareto) 1903 xx,
   3, 4, 13–18, 29–30, 32–40, 55, 62, 76–7,
   117n
*Lezioni di scienze economica razionale e
   sperimentale* (Rovigo) 27
Liberal Party 76
liberal utopia 76
liberalism xxi, xxv, 2, 76
Livingston, A. 117
Livy 66–7
Lloyd George, D. 120
logic 56, 62, 89, 103, 108
logical and non-logical action xii, xiii, xiv,
   xvii–xviii, xxi, 15, 42–3, 57
logico–experimental method 6, 14–16,
   29–36, 40, 42, 44, 45, 46–7, 48–9, 56, 89,
   90

Machiavelli, Niccolo 18, 75
Manuale di economia politica (Pareto)
   1906 xxi, 3, 4, 5, 6, 7–11, 13–17, 21, 25,
   76–7, 94
Manuel d'économie politique (Pareto)
   1909 xxi, 3, 4, 5, 6, 7, 9, 10, 21, 25–8,
   94
Marshall, Alfred 6, 110
Marx and Marxism xi–xiii, xvii, xix, xxi,
   15, 29, 32–5, 55, 72, 73–4, 117n, 118n
mathematics 1, 6–10, 42, 46, 55, 77, 82–3,
   84–7, 90, 93, 95–8, 101, 103, 107, 113, 115
   analysis 6–10
   economics 2, 5, 7–12, 19, 89–90, 93, 96,
      100, 106–10, 115
   statistics 10–13, 102
Maxwell, J. 106
mechanics xi, 7, 8, 9, 10, 86, 89–90, 96–9
   hereditary 83–4
Menger, Karl 41
military, the 64, 65, 119n
Mill, J.S. 50
Mitchell, W.C. 114
modern society 61
   analogy with Roman Empire 63–4
   crystallisation 73–4
   Fascism 62, 69–72
   First World War 64–6, 67–8
monetary dynamics 113
monetary systems 7
money 7, 68, 101
monopoly 7, 9, 21–2, 24–6, 28, 76, 94
Moor, H.L. 110–13

Moore, G.   110–13
moral sciences   91
Morishima, M.   117
Mussolini, Benito   70, 120n
myths   51

Napoleon I   71
Napoleon III   71
nationalism   2, 47
natural phenomena   98
natural rights   31, 118n
natural sciences   41, 82, 97
Nero   46
non-logical actions   xii, xiii, xiv–xxi, 15,
   43–5, 49, 57, 86

ophelimity   7, 9, 22, 26, 28, 52, 94, 107,
   113, 118n
Osorio, A.   93

pacifism   62
Pantaleoni, M.   xxv, 5, 6, 56
Pareto, Vilfredo
   and Fascism   62, 69–72
   as a scientist   75
   as impartial theoretician and
      scientist   75, 82–90
   as practical and theoretical politician   1,
      75–82
   as sociologist   xxv, 13–20, 41–59, 66–74,
      75
   family   1–2
   law of income distribution   10–12
   major works
      *Le Cours de' économie
         politique*   2–11, 13–14, 16–17,
         24–5, 41, 52, 75–7, 82, 86, 93–4
      *Economie mathématique,
         in Encyclopédie des sciences
         mathématiques*   3–6
      Fatti e teorie   3, 14, 64
      Manuale di economia politica   3–17,
         21, 25, 76–7, 94
      Manuel d'économie politique   4–10,
         21, 25, 28, 94
      *Il mito virtuista e la litteratura
         immorale*   3, 4, 13, 18
      *Le Mythe vertuiste et la littérature
         immorale*   3, 4
      Les Systèmes socialistes   3–4, 13–18,
         29–33, 38–40, 55, 76–7

      Trasformazione della democrazia   3,
         4, 18
      Trattato di sociologia generale   3, 4,
         14–19, 29–45, 50, 52,
         (*French translation: Traité de
            sociologie générale*)   56, 61, 79–81
      political views of   70–2
      works of   2–4, 13–14
   patriotism   47
   peace   65–6, 76
Pearson, K.   101
perfect numbers   46–7
persistence of aggregates   16, 17, 47, 62–3
philology   15, 42
philosophers and philosophy   2, 5, 10, 15,
   20, 35, 51, 53, 57, 85, 89
Philosophie des Als Ob (Vaihinger)   57
physical sciences   2, 4, 5, 82, 84, 86, 87, 89,
   91, 106
physics   1, 8, 10, 41, 58, 84, 97–9, 106
Plato   34, 50
pleasure   9, 57
plutocracy   62–4, 69–72, 78, 80
Poincaré, Jules   9, 58
political economy   13, 41, 121n
politics   1, 5, 13, 41, 70–2, 75–82, 95,
   121n
Polybius   64
population   7, 11
poverty   xxiii, 31, 70
power   18, 38, 63, 65, 68–9, 121n
prices   8–9, 21–7, 41, 66, 94, 100, 101–2,
   107, 111, 113, 114
Principe (Machiavelli)   75
private property   xxi, 30, 36, 54
privatisation   xxii
probability, theory of   11–12, 105–7, 110
production   xii, xiii, 7, 8, 21–8, 32–4, 41,
   77, 93, 94, 111, 113
   coefficients   7–9, 26–7, 94, 110–11
profit   xii, xiv–xv, xvii, 9, 110
protectionism   xxii, 73, 76–7
Proudhon, P.   32
Pythagoras   46

reality   6, 56–8, 61, 68, 77, 80, 82, 84, 87,
   101, 103, 105, 110, 112
reason   62
refugees   78
relativity, theory of   83
religion   xii–xiii, xviii, 18, 37, 46, 47, 48,
   52–3, 72, 78, 85, 117n

rent 41, 93
rentiers 77, 120n
residues xviii, xx–xxiii, 15–19, 44, 45–57, 62–4, 67, 70, 73, 86
   fiction 57
   hypothesis- 57
Resto del carlino 66, 68
revolution xvii, xxii–xxiii, 39, 61, 63, 69–70, 73
Ricardo, David 7
Rivista di politica economia xxiv–xxv
Rivista d'Italia 66, 121n
Rivista italiana di sociologia 4
Robespierre, Maximilien 53, 71
Roman Empire xxii, 36, 37, 43, 53, 61–4, 66, 71, 73, 119n
Roos, C.F. 101–2, 106
Roosevelt, F.D. 80
ruling class xi, xvii, xxii, 62–3, 70, 78
Russia 64, 67

Saint–Simon, Claude-Henri 34, 35
Sallust 69
savings 54, 66
schools of thought from Pareto's theories 91–6
Schultz, H. 114
Schumpeter, J.A. xi, xiv, xvi–xvii, xx, xxi–xxiv, 117n
science 2, 4–6, 10, 20, 51–2, 56, 57–9, 73, 81–3, 86–9, 92, 95, 96–7, 100, 103, 115
Scientia 65
Secolo 67, 71
Second World War 18–19, 79
selection 34
Sensini, Guido 56, 93, 95
sentiments xii, xiv, 16, 36–7, 44, 46–9, 51, 53, 61, 69, 73, 119n
sexual impulse xx, 16, 49–50
sociability 48
social action 14, 106–7
social classes xi, xvii, xxii, 36–9, 47, 52, 54, 62–3, 70, 78
social cycles 55–6, 59
social dynamic 55, 59
social equilibrium xi, xiii, xvii, xxiii, 17, 40, 44, 48, 58
social evolution 55–6, 58–9
social heterogeneity 61–2
social phenomena 14, 17, 37–40, 41, 45, 50–5, 57, 59, 69–72, 121n

social realities 39–40, 41, 42, 45, 57, 80, 81, 83, 109, 115
social research 14, 82–90
social sciences xi, xiii, 2, 5, 13–14, 19, 41, 42, 82, 84, 87, 89, 92
social utility 18, 51–2
socialism xiii, xx–xxiii, xxiv–xxv, 2, 7, 18, 29–40, 47, 64, 70, 71, 72, 73, 74, 78, 117n, 121n
sociological theories 8, 14–20, 29–40, 41–59, 81, 91–2
   criticisms of Pareto's 92–5
sociology xi, xvii, xviii–xx, xxiii, 1, 8, 14–20, 29, 41, 42, 55, 57, 59, 69, 83, 86–7, 90, 92, 95, 108, 121n
   synthesis of economics and 87
solidarity 31
Sorel, G. 16, 18, 51, 77–8, 79–80
Soviet Union xiii, xxiv
Spartacists 69
Spencer, H. 17, 50, 74
Spinoza, Baruch xviii
stability 16, 17, 38, 47, 64, 70, 72–3, 101
state control of industry and public services 72
statistics 1, 10–13, 92, 101, 102, 105, 109–12
   research 112–15
stock exchange 7
stock market 114
Suetonius 46
superstructure xii–xiii, xvii, xix
supply 106, 110, 111
surplus value 33
Swedberg, R. 117
Switzerland 65, 76
system transformation xvii

takeover xv–xvi
taxation 30, 65, 72, 95, 101
Taylor, J.S. 101
teetotallers 78
Temps 71
Thatcher, Margaret xxii
Thomas, Saint 50
time, functions of 98–101, 103–4, 107, 111
Tinbergen, J. 102
Tobin, J. xv
trade 7, 21–4, 26–7, 107, 111
   international 7, 9, 77, 93, 94–5
trade unions xii, 2, 39

Traité de sociologie générale (Pareto)
1919 3, 42–53, 61, 62–4, 65, 120n
transfer of goods 76–7
Trasformazione della democrazia (Pareto)
1921 3, 4, 18–19, 69
Trattato di sociologia generale (Pareto)
1916 xviii, xx, xxiii, xxiv, 3, 4, 14, 16,
17–19, 29–30, 40, 56, 59, 79, 80, 81
Tutankhamun 43–4

unemployment 68, 114
uniformity 34–5, 48
United States of America 79
utility xii, xiv, xvii, 7, 9, 16–18, 51–2, 57, 113

Vaihinger, Hans 57
value xiii, 33, 41, 55
vegetarians 78
Versailles Treaty 67
Vico, G. 17, 54
virtual movements 51
virtuism 49

virtuosity 18
Vita interazionale 65
Volt, M. 70–1
Volterra, Vito 9, 90, 97–101, 105, 108

wages 7, 11–12, 41
Walras, L. xi, xiv, 2, 6, 7, 9, 10, 21, 22–3,
28, 41, 42, 52, 55, 58, 86, 89, 93, 94, 96,
97, 102, 108, 110–12
war xxii–xxiii, 18–19, 64–6, 67–8, 79
wealth 32, 63, 77, 107
destruction of 76–7
distribution 33–4, 38
Weber, Max xi, xiii, xxv, 117n
West Germany xvi
Western Europe 61, 63, 69
see also specific countries
Wilson, Woodrow 67

Yntema, T.O. 93

Zuccharini, M. 121

98500496R00089

Made in the USA
Columbia, SC
26 June 2018